WENDY HAYES

Escape *from* Egypt

A PATHWAY TO FREEDOM FOR WOMEN

Ark House Press
arkhousepress.com

© 2022 Wendy Hayes

All rights reserved. No part of this publication may be reproduced, stored ina retrieval system, or transmitted in any form or by any means, electronic, mechanical, photocopying or otherwise, without the prior written consent of the publisher. Short extracts may be used for review purposes.

Scripture quotations marked TPT are from The Passion Translation®. Copyright © 2017, 2018 by Passion & Fire Ministries, Inc. Used by permission. All rights reserved. ThePassionTranslation.com.

Scripture quotations taken from the New American Standard Bible® (NASB), Copyright © 1960, 1962, 1963, 1968, 1971, 1972, 1973, 1975, 1977, 1995 by The Lockman Foundation. Used by permission. www.Lockman.org

Scripture quotations marked (NLT) are taken from the Holy Bible, New Living Translation, copyright © 1996, 2004, 2015 by Tyndale House Foundation. Used by permission of Tyndale House Publishers, Inc., Carol Stream, Illinois 60188. All rights reserved.

All Scripture quotations, unless otherwise indicated, are taken from the Holy Bible, New International Version®, NIV®. Copyright ©1973, 1978, 1984, 2011 by Biblica, Inc.™ Used by permission of Zondervan. All rights reserved worldwide. www.zondervan.com The "NIV" and "New International Version" are trademarks registered in the United States Patent and Trademark Office by Biblica, Inc.™

Scripture quotations marked (AMP) are taken from the Amplified Bible, Copyright © 2015 by The Lockman Foundation. Used by permission.

Scripture taken from the New King James Version®. Copyright © 1982 by Thomas Nelson. Used by permission. All rights reserved.

[Scripture quotations are from] New Revised Standard Version Bible, copyright © 1989 National Council of the Churches of Christ in the United States of America. Used by permission. All rights reserved worldwide.

Cataloguing in Publication Data:
Title: Escape From Egypt
ISBN: 978-0-6454926-0-6 (pbk)
Subjects: Domestic Violence; Church Culture; Biography;
Other Authors/Contributors: Hayes, Wendy

Design by initiateagency.com

DEDICATION

I dedicate this book to my children, Isaac, Jordan, Sarah, Teresa, Levi, and their partners. I'm in awe of your wisdom, love, and the exceptional way you do life.

Special love to my grandchildren, Khoa, Wyatt, Oakley, Tahlie and Kairo, and those on the way.

ACKNOWLEDGMENTS

To my husband, Ray, you have supported me in every venture and shown me what true love looks like. Your belief in me picks me up when the going gets tough. I'm forever grateful.

A special thank you to my sister Jo. Your prayers, wisdom, and encouragement have been vital to this journey.

To my friends and prayer partners, this project wouldn't exist without you. I love doing life with you as we pursue Him and His Kingdom.

A huge thank you to Renée. You are a truly gifted editor. I've learned so much as we've worked on this project together.

TABLE OF CONTENTS

Dedication iii
Acknowledgments v
Endorsements ix
Introduction xiii
CHAPTER ONE: From Eve to Egypt 1
CHAPTER TWO: Religion Kills 14
CHAPTER THREE: Freedom from Shame 30
CHAPTER FOUR: Freedom from Control 50
CHAPTER FIVE: Freedom from Guilt 64
CHAPTER SIX: Freedom from Intimidation 79
CHAPTER SEVEN: Realms of Authority 97
CHAPTER EIGHT: Kingdom Marriages 118
CHAPTER NINE: Eve in the Promised Land 141
APPENDIX: Domestic Violence 154
Notes 157
About the Author 161

ENDORSEMENTS

This is a wonderful book that speaks to my heart. It is both informative and transformative. For those of us impacted by trauma, the challenge to growth and change can be a difficult journey. We can find ourselves trapped behind prison walls that keep us from true freedom.

Wendy takes us on a journey that helps us explore our core beliefs on submission and other important issues by examining whether they are based on biblical truth or church practices that can create oppression rather than freedom in Christ.

Research, personal experience, and scriptural truth combine to bring healing and release to women, including reflective moments with the Holy Spirit. Be encouraged as you are led to discover greater freedom and growth into all Christ has for you.

Helen Meyer
Director Careforce Lifekeys International

In *Escape from Egypt*, Wendy Hayes brings a "now" word for the Church. She calls out the religious spirit masquerading as Kingdom authority that's cloaked countless women in fear and shame. Wendy brings her considerable knowledge and expertise as a Christian Counsellor to bear in this must-read. It's time for the Church to confront this religious spirit, and *Escape from Egypt* is a great way to begin. I highly recommend you grab a copy and start the journey.

Dawna De Silva
Author, Speaker, and Overseer,
Bethel Sozo Founder & Co-Leader

I have the honour to call Wendy Hayes my friend. She is an anointed wife, mother, counsellor, teacher, intercessor, leader, and more. She is led by the Holy Spirit and full of His wisdom, revelation, and power. She writes from a place of transparency, humility, and love about the journey she has been on and empowers others to experience the same freedom.

Isaiah 60:1 says, "Arise [from the depression and prostration in which circumstances have kept you - rise to a new life]! Shine [be radiant with the glory and brilliance of the Lord]; for your light has come, and the glory of the Lord has risen upon you".

There is an invitation from our Heavenly Father to arise and shine. And with this invitation comes His provision and empowering to leave the past behind and step into all He has prepared for us. We are His precious daughters, called, anointed, and appointed by Him, not only to walk in freedom for ourselves but also to bring His love and healing to our world.

Wendy's beautifully written book is a God-given tool to help us on this healing journey. Wendy is living Isaiah 60. She shines, and you can too! I highly recommend this book.

Jenny Cornish

I have known Wendy for six years. We instantly connected, and I enjoyed Wendy's insight into the prophetic and inner healing realm. Wendy has incredible insight and gifting in the supernatural and practical realm of inner healing. She has developed her own inner healing training program, which encapsulates her unique style, gifting, knowledge, and divine wisdom.

This has naturally led her to write *Escape from Egypt*, which is a book that I can't recommend highly enough. It's full of prophetic insight, wisdom, and years of training. It will set you free from the things that have held you back and bring you deeper into your divine calling.

Jane Marquis

I first met Wendy in my early 20s as a young youth pastor's wife and lover of the local church. As I've wrestled over the years to make sense of my own journey and that of others, time with Wendy has marked many moments where I have found freedom and healing as I encountered truth and a deeper connection with God.

Her book, *Escape from Egypt*, echoes so much of my own journey and brings essential truths that need to be central to every Christian's experience with the Gospel.

Wendy reminds us that life is designed to be in relationship and not rules and that it's truth, encountered in every part of our heart and life, that leads us out into freedom.

Kirstin Geerling

INTRODUCTION

Freedom! Don't you just love that word? It's so deep in our core that world wars are fought to protect it. The United Nations established a charter of fundamental human rights to protect the freedom of individuals because we recognise it's foundational to our wellbeing.

Ponder the words of William Wallace for a moment:

> "Fight and you may die. Run, and you'll live… at least a while. And dying in your beds, many years from now, would you be willin' to trade all the days, from this day to that, for one chance, just one chance, to come back here and tell our enemies that they may take our lives, but they'll never take… our freedom!"[1]

Freedom is central to the Gospel message because it's central to God's plan for humanity. It's the culture of the Kingdom and the environment we were designed to live in and from. In the same way our bodies are designed for oxygen and will fight to breathe, our souls are meant to live in freedom, and we will fight to gain and keep it.

For me, freedom feels like riding a horse through the open countryside; no fences, no people; just me and my horse in nature. The beach is another place I feel free. There's something about the expanse of the ocean that brings me into a place of deep rest. What does freedom look like for you?

We're made for freedom, to rule and reign with God for the good of all the Earth. God gave Adam and Eve authority and freedom of choice.

> "Then God said, "Let us make human beings in our image, to be like us. They will reign over the fish in the sea, the birds in the sky, the livestock, all the wild animals on the Earth, and the small animals that scurry along the ground."
>
> So God created human beings in his own image. In the image of God he created them; male and female he created them. Then God blessed them and said, "Be fruitful and multiply. Fill the Earth and govern it. Reign over the fish in the sea, the birds in the sky, and all the animals that scurry along the ground." (Genesis 1:26-28 NLT)

When humanity fell, everything changed. There was a transfer of authority that led to our captivity. People went from ruling with God to being under the rule and authority of the Kingdom of darkness. Jesus came to take back that authority, and He's given it to those who follow Him. He's set us free from the power of sin, death, and the oppression we've experienced as slaves. Jesus has restored our dignity and authority, giving us back to our true identities as children of God. Now it's time for us to take hold of this truth.

Power and wealth are sought by many because of the perceived freedom attached. One of the reasons life on Earth is so difficult is that we're not operating from the authority for which we were designed. The problem is that when power is concentrated in a select few, oppression of the many is invariably the case. Moreover, both oppressors and oppressed are not aligned with God's Kingdom order. The Father intends us to carry His delegated authority and extend His Kingdom rule over the Earth—together.

Our adversary is cunning. He goes by one name but comes in many guises – fear, shame, guilt, and accusation, to name a few. The Bible says he appears as an angel of light. He cloaks himself in religion and reason, using them to enslave and imprison. Many of us live in slavery without knowing it, and if you don't know you're in captivity—why would you ever seek to be free?

THE STRUGGLE FOR FREEDOM

I'm a professional Christian counsellor with a Masters in Community Counselling and over ten years in private practice. My goal is to help Christians appropriate the Gospel into their everyday lives – to walk in the fullness of freedom that Jesus purchased through His sacrifice. My pursuit of healing and freedom for my clients has led me to study childhood trauma and abuse. I've observed, time and again, when clients struggle to experience God's love, His presence and hear His voice, there is a history of childhood abuse. I've come to understand that abuse and neglect in childhood profoundly impact our ability to receive the love of God and walk in freedom.

I've walked with God for thirty years and have been in church leadership for most of that time. I work primarily with women who feel a blockage in their relationship with God and struggle to find freedom from emotional pain. For those who are married, far too many seek to be perfect to avoid triggering their husband's anger or disapproval. Over the years, I've witnessed a pattern of re-victimisation, though I've only recently discovered the language for what I'm seeing.

I see Christians struggling to submit to authority while holding on to their freedom. I work with many clients who are oppressed, feeling trapped by family, work, or church authorities. Oppression is defined as "the prolonged cruel, or unjust exercise of authority." [2] We can guard against such abuse, and it begins with understanding what Kingdom authority is and what it isn't.

KINGDOM AUTHORITY—WHAT IT IS AND WHAT IT ISN'T!

It's why I'm writing this book. I want to help expose the subtle lies that keep women in bondage and under the yoke of slavery. We can't change what we don't know. So many of us, myself included, have been deceived into taking on this yoke. No one's immune, and there's no shame attached; only healing, restoration, and abundant life. I've worked with hundreds of sincere Christian women whose freedom and authority has been ripped away, and I'm tired of it. The Apostle Paul felt the same way as he wrote to the Galatian church.

> "Now we're no longer living like slaves under the law, but we enjoy being God's very own sons and daughters! And because we're his, we can access everything our Father has—for we are heirs because of what God has done!" (Galatians 5:7 TPT)

I was 24 years old when I started walking with God. I had no church, or religious background, was pretty independent and leaned toward feminism— although I never referred to myself as a feminist. I remember my outrage watching my sister iron her boyfriend's shirts. Everything in me wanted to shout, "Don't his arms work? Why is that your job?" So, you can imagine my response to scriptures telling wives to submit to their husbands! It didn't make sense to me, but I'd embarked on a faith journey with my whole heart, and I took God's Word seriously. I started seeking the Lord for His perspective on the entire issue of submission, not just in families but also in the church.

I found it easy to trust God and believe He had my best interests at heart, so submitting to His authority was no big deal. On the other hand, submitting to people was an entirely different story. I was shocked to learn I was expected to submit to my pastor and follow his guidance regarding decisions about my life.

I started swinging between extremes, submitting without question or shutting out every voice other than God's. I wanted a formula to apply to every situation but discovered the subtle danger attached to this kind of thinking. We have an enemy who uses Scripture against us, and we need both wisdom and Godly counsel to walk in the truth and freedom that the Lord has for us.

I want to draw clear lines between Kingdom authority and the oppression unleashed when we yield our authority to the enemy. Our enemy seeks to keep us from our full potential, and one of his schemes is to keep us oppressed and contained through control.

In his book *Breaking Intimidation*, John Bevere explains:

> *"If you don't walk in your God-given authority, someone will take it from you and use it against you ".*[3]

He goes on to say:

> *"It is important to understand that there is a dwelling place or position in the spirit that we hold as believers in Jesus. With this position comes authority. This authority is what the enemy wants. If he can get us to yield our God-given authority, he will take it and use it against us. This not only affects us but those entrusted to our care"* [4]

Jesus said that the truth would set us free. I aim to help dispel some of the theological and doctrinal extremes that undermine our God-given authority and lead to captivity. Either the accuser will oppress you, or you will stand in your authority and rule over him. When we've been living under oppression, we must be re-positioned. It's like the Israelites moving from slavery and oppression in Egypt to taking their rightful place in the Promised Land, where they were victorious over their enemies.

GOD'S PEOPLE IN BONDAGE

The Israelites spent 430 years in captivity. Their Egyptian masters made life miserable, oppressing them with back-breaking, soul-crushing labour.

> "So the Egyptians worked the people of Israel without mercy. They made their lives bitter, forcing them to mix mortar and make bricks and do all the work in the fields. They were ruthless in all their demands." (Exodus 1:13,14 NLT)

The slave drivers aimed to wear the people down and weaken them to the point of hopelessness and despair. The Children of Israel came to see themselves as powerless against their oppressors. A once strong and highly favoured family took on a negative identity, and generations lived and died under this falsehood.

Imagine never having the freedom to make choices about your life – where you live or what you do. Imagine never having the opportunity to build a life for yourself or leave an inheritance for your children. Imagine not having time to play with your children or dream with them about their future. Imagine waking every day to another day of hard work, beatings, and abuse. Generation after generation at the mercy of their oppressors; it's hard to imagine the magnitude of collective suffering.

The story of the Israelites is a helpful metaphor for living in bondage to an oppressor. Jesus often used parables to explain spiritual concepts because they're relatable. Just as there came a moment when God set His people free and led them out of Egypt, He's leading Christian women out of oppression.

A new picture emerges as we look at Scripture through the lens of love and address issues that work against freedom. An over-emphasis on certain doctrines combined with the prevalence of childhood abuse and neglect have greyed the lines between Godly submission and the containment that comes through oppression. Sadly, many of us have felt trapped, believing it to be God who put us there.

I've helped Christian women find freedom and healing for over 20 years. As part of my master's degree, I researched the impact of Christian church culture on the re-victimisation of women.

A study by Hana Al-Modallal in 2016 found that those traumatised by childhood abuse are more likely to be victims of sexual assault or domestic violence in adulthood.[5] They called it *re-victimisation*. Many survivors of abuse and assault ask, "Why does this keep happening to me? Is there something wrong with me?". They observe many of their friends and relatives having no similar experience, while they have repeated incidents throughout their lives.

The Australian Bureau of Statistics Personal Safety Study 2016 confirms my experience as a counsellor.[6] Most of my clients who've experienced domestic violence as adults have a childhood history of abuse. The research backs up their lived experience, confirming re-victimisation as a genuine issue.

"Compared to their counterparts, risk of severe physical partner violence was three-fold greater in women who experienced childhood physical violence and five-fold greater among those who witnessed mother-to-father violence. Victims of childhood maltreatment may encounter social and personal problems that increase their vulnerability to violence in adulthood." [7]

One of the ways childhood traumas impact a person is the inability to connect with and regulate their emotions. Dissociation is a term used to describe the disconnection from emotions that often accompany trauma.[8] Dissociation makes it more difficult for women to feel the emotional and physical internal signals that a person or situation is unsafe.[9]

DISEMPOWERING CHURCH CULTURE

As my research progressed, it emerged that a woman's vulnerability to domestic violence increases if she's been immersed in conservative church culture.

I was shocked and horrified to discover the mindsets of powerlessness learned through childhood abuse were being reinforced in church. Rather than finding healing and freedom, many women were taught the way to please God was to surrender their rights and freedom to their husbands and church leaders. I'd always believed the church to be a place of healing and restoration. But now, I saw first-hand the negative impact of a religious church culture on abuse victims.

Fifteen years ago, I heard the Lord say, "The Church is in Egypt". I didn't understand what He meant because I was taught that the Israelites in Egypt was a picture of life before salvation. But He continued, "Egypt is My people in bondage".

I didn't understand at the time, but little by little, the revelation unfurled— that most of us are yet to experience the true freedom God intends. Freedom from the oppression of control and freedom from physical and mental illness oppression. Instead, there's a spirit at work enslaving many of God's people. The pages of this book will focus on the implications for women; however, the effects aren't limited to a specific gender, age, or denomination.

God is bringing women into freedom by releasing truth to expose the deception they've experienced. The tables are turning; women are coming out from under shame and captivity to walk in their destiny and trample the works of Satan. God destined, right back in the garden of Eden, that the descendants of Eve would crush the head of the serpent, and we are that generation. Shame came upon Eve in the garden, but God doesn't leave us in shame; He takes us into glory.

FROM SHAME TO GLORY

Colossians 1:27 tells us that we have the hope of glory. In this context, *glory* denotes honour, renown, and high esteem. It's the opposite of shame. Women have a vital role in ushering in the Kingdom of God, and now is the time to receive your breakthrough and healing. Do you want to break through the containment lines and live in the freedom of all Christ made you to be? We're the radical ones who know no bounds, who will search for the truth and break through the traditions and containment of past generations.

We're entering a season of momentous shift for the women of God. God is leading us out of Egypt – out from under the oppression that has kept us bound. Out from under the shame of the curse and into the glory of our redemption. This book will address the areas and issues that have kept us in Egypt. We'll look at the impact of trauma, imbalanced religious teaching, and cultures of oppression. We'll explore how they've disempowered women and led generations to believe Egypt is the Promised Land.

As we align with God in this battle for our freedom, the struggle itself will strengthen and equip us to set others free. As we partner with God, the enemy's plans will come into sharp focus. No longer fighting shadows, we'll get him clear in our sights and, with swords sharpened, lead the way.

The Gospel of Matthew tells us that the last will be first, and the first shall be last. His words are pertinent right now. God's justice is being released on the Earth as He brings women out of shame into glory. The tables will turn in the coming days as the oppressed rise up to take down their oppressor. Not just for themselves but for all those who have been held captive.

HOW TO USE THIS BOOK

It's not my intention to give you rules to live by or formulas to follow. Instead, I want to provoke you to question the status quo, journey with

Holy Spirit, and let Him speak into your life. If you, like me, have struggled to be under authority without going to extremes, this book is for you.

All truth is held in tension, and when a particular element of Scripture is taken out of context and used without balance, it no longer reflects the heart of God. Many people comment on the apparent contradictions in the Bible. These aren't errors on the part of God – they happen because the Bible is written for humans who tend toward rules and extremes. God in His wisdom made allowances so that the extremes are tempered.

We'll study how the enemy has used manipulation and intimidation to steal our authority and use it against us. Shame impacts all of us, keeping us from reaching our potential. When we learn to recognise true Kingdom authority and leadership characteristics, we're well placed to identify oppressive power and choose freedom.

I've written this book because I know God doesn't want you to live powerless and hidden. Rather, He's calling you to arise and walk in the glory of everything he created you to be.

I encourage you to spend time in the prayers at the end of each chapter. It's an essential step in renewing your mind with truth. Holy Spirit will help you take what you've learned and apply it to your specific circumstances. So please resist the temptation to skip them. Instead, allow them to bring you into an encounter with God — the source of our healing and freedom.

Have a pen and paper handy as you pray. Then sit and listen for His response. Sometimes God answers immediately in the form of thoughts, impressions, or images. Write down what you sense He is revealing to you.

If you don't get anything immediately, don't worry. Answers may come hours or even days later. They may come directly to you, through something you read, or other people. The important thing is to expect Him to answer. He is a good Father who delights in speaking with His children.

Let's begin.

CHAPTER ONE

From Eve to Egypt

The story of Eve fascinates me. The Genesis account of the Fall is often relegated to Sunday school, but it has much to teach us about our destiny as women. We will look at the consequences of Eve's decision in the Garden of Eden and how it's impacted women throughout history. Jesus promised that the truth would set us free. Getting free from oppression relies heavily on our ability to discern what's from God and what isn't.

In the book of Genesis, God created a beautiful garden; He put humanity in charge and gave them dominion over all creation. It's important to note that God gave *both* Adam and Eve authority. Authority is the right and power to make decisions. Authority and empowerment go hand in hand, with studies showing emotional wellbeing is linked to feeling empowered.

"Then God said, "Let us make mankind in our image, in our likeness, so that they may rule over the fish in the sea and the birds in the sky, over the livestock and all the wild animals, and over all the creatures that move along the ground."

So God created mankind in his own image, in the image of God he created them; male and female he created them.

God blessed them and said to them, "Be fruitful and increase in number; fill the Earth and subdue it. Rule over the fish in the sea and the birds in the sky and over every living creature that moves on the ground." (Genesis 1:26-28 NIV)

Adam and Eve had it made in the garden; they enjoyed an intimate relationship with God. He met their every need and gave them a defining role on the Earth. Then Eve decided to trust the serpent over God. We all know the story; there were two trees in the garden; one was the tree of life, and the other was the tree of the knowledge of good and evil. God told Adam and Eve not to eat from the tree of the knowledge of good and evil and that if they did, they would die. Then Eve did the one thing God said not to do, and the rest is history.

A TALE OF TWO KINGDOMS

A *kingdom* is the realm of authority of a ruler.[1] The two trees represent two kingdoms in the Genesis narrative, those of God and Satan.

Satan wanted to be worshipped like God. The tree of the knowledge of good and evil represents a religious system of rules, performance, and trying to navigate right and wrong—a counterfeit to God's Kingdom. Satan wanted to be worshipped like God and gain authority over the Earth, so he tricked Eve into handing over her God-given power.

> "Don't you realise that grace frees you to choose your own master? But choose carefully, for you surrender yourself to become a servant—bound to the one you choose to obey. If you choose to love sin, it will become your master, and it will own you and reward you with death. But if you choose to love and obey God, he will lead you into perfect righteousness." (Romans 6:16 TPT)

By aligning themselves with the Kingdom of darkness, Adam and Eve rejected God's authority, enslaving humanity under Satan's rule.

The tree of life represents God's Kingdom. He wanted a family relationship where love, rather than laws, governed behaviour. According to Strong's Concordance, the word used in reference to the tree of life means "living, alive, flowing, fresh, reviving, sustenance, revival, renewal, relatives and community".[2] That sounds so much better than knowledge, doesn't it? God's Kingdom brings life and sustenance. And note that the word's *relatives* and *community* are related to life; God's way is all about connection through a loving relationship.

KINGDOM AUTHORITY

Authority is God's idea; it's meant for our good and never intended to be harmful or restrictive. Everything in the Kingdom is motivated by love. Anything that originates with God is designed to be an instrument to care for people. Jesus modelled and taught the characteristics of Kingdom leadership. (Matthew 20:25-28) He showed the disciples that Kingdom leadership and authority differed from their lived experience. Freedom begins with knowing what it feels like when we're under God's authority. When oppression has been our normal, it's hard to imagine another way.

What does the word *authority* bring to mind? Do you find yourself tensing, bracing for something unpleasant? Many of us have had negative dealings with authority figures leaving us bruised and disillusioned. Yet, our disappointment reveals that deep down, we know it shouldn't be that way. Jesus made a clear distinction between God's use of authority and how it's misapplied.

> "Jesus, knowing their thoughts, called them to his side and said, "Kings and those with great authority in this world rule oppressively over their subjects, like tyrants. But this is not your calling. You will lead by a completely different model. The greatest one among you will live as the one who is called to serve others, because the greatest honour and authority is reserved for the one with the heart of a servant. For even the Son of Man did not come expecting to be served but to serve and give his life in exchange for the salvation of many." (Matthew 20:25-28 TPT)

Jesus told his disciples not to lord it over the people they led. 'Lording it over' means to overpower or master.[3] This type of leadership leaves people scarred and wary of all authority figures. Authority is oppressive when used to meet the needs of leaders at the expense of those under their authority.

Unfortunately, we don't have to look too far for examples. Think governments where the leaders and officials profit through corruption, living extravagant lifestyles while their people suffer in abject poverty. When people have no power of choice or destiny, they are under oppression.

Jesus explained that in God's Kingdom, the purpose of leadership is to *serve* those you lead. Authority is exercised to enhance the wellbeing of others and is sacrificial. Healthy parenting is an example of this kind of leadership. Mums and Dads use their authority to protect their children from harm and empower them to succeed in life. They're practising servant leadership and kingdom authority to serve the next generation.

REST

Jesus came to give us *rest*. Have you ever stopped and thought about that? I see worn-out Christians, convinced they're not doing enough, believing Jesus is the one pushing them. Striving for approval isn't rest; it's work. Jesus should be the one we run to when we're weary, but many Christians run from Him because they believe He's got more for them to do!

> "Are you weary, carrying a heavy burden? Come to me.
> I will refresh your life, for I am your oasis. Simply join

your life with mine. Learn my ways, and you'll discover that I'm gentle, humble, easy to please. You will find refreshment and **rest** in me. For all that I require of you will be pleasant and easy to bear." (Matthew 11:28-30 TPT)

Jesus is nothing like the taskmasters of Egypt. In His rest, striving ceases, and there's the freedom to simply *be*. Jesus doesn't stand behind you with a list of things to do—rest is His idea! The kind of rest Jesus is talking about is more than a holiday or spending the day in bed; it's a way of living. What does rest look like for you? I love going to the movies or curling up with a good book by the fire. I have friends who love nothing more than a hike or bike ride. You may be working hard physically, but you're rested because you're doing what you love and have the freedom to choose. It's *rest for your soul.*

We enter deep soul rest through faith in the finished work of the Cross. There's nothing for you to do; you're accepted just as you are. Acceptance isn't based on your righteousness but the righteousness of Christ. Once positioned in love, acceptance, and rest, the love of God pulls you toward the good works prepared for you. The Holy Spirit leads and guides—He will never coerce or force – it's not in His nature. You can freely enter His presence; knowing what Jesus did on the Cross is enough.

The book of Hebrews equates the Promised Land with God's rest for His people. The Lord led the Israelites out of servitude in Egypt into freedom and rest. He provided everything they needed, and all He asked was that they trust him, move forward, and possess the land. The writer of Hebrews tells us that it was unbelief, ultimately in God's goodness, that kept them from entering their Promised Land for forty years.

> "As we enter into God's faith-rest life, we cease from our own works, just as God celebrates his finished works and rests in them. So then we must be eager to experience this faith-rest life, so that no one falls short by following the same pattern of doubt and unbelief." (Hebrews 4:10-11 TPT)

Stop working to earn God's favour – you already have it! God is pleased with you when you believe Him. Like Abraham, whose righteousness was credited to him by his faith, we're positioned in perfect peace with the Father when we trust His love and grace.

In Biblical times, yokes were used to harness oxen together. They signify a joining together. Think of being yoked in terms of looking to the other person as your gauge of what to do and the direction you should be heading. In the joining, we take on the responsibilities they want us to carry. A typical example of this is when a parent wants their child to pursue a particular career. The adult child feels the pull from the parent to choose this vocation, even though it may not be what they desire or are gifted by God to do. Some will not come under such a yoke or feel burdened by their parent's wishes, but others will feel the full weight.

Jesus invites us to take on His yoke because it's easy, and His burden is light. He knows us intimately, including our gifts and current capacity. We're safe when yoked with Him. If we look to please Him rather than people, He'll direct us to love others well, love ourselves well, and fulfil the good works He's planned for us to do. So if you feel weary and burdened, if guilt and shame weigh you down, it's time to look at the yokes you've taken on.

Jesus was angry with the Pharisees because they placed heavy burdens on the Israelites. They were guilty of misrepresenting God to the people. This same dynamic is still at work today. When we take off every yoke except that of Jesus, it leads us into rest. His yoke fits well because it only asks us to do what He knows we can do. He releases grace (supernatural empowerment) for us to do the things He asks. That's why His yoke is easy, and His burden is light (Matt 11:28-30).

WHAT TYPE OF LEADER WAS JESUS?

I hope we can agree God isn't a slavedriver. He's a good father. He cares for His children, and He wants us to rest in Him. But if our parents, church leaders, and others in authority looked like the Egyptians, it's hard to believe in a good God. Jesus said, "If you've seen me, you've seen the Father" (John 14:9). So, let's spend some time looking at the way Jesus led His disciples.

In Jesus, we see a leader who gave His life for the benefit of His followers. He didn't use His position for selfish gain or to be served. Instead, He taught His disciples the principles of the Kingdom of God and sent them out to do the same works He did. Jesus modelled self-sacrificing love toward His friends. Not only did He wash their feet in humility, but He also suffered humiliation, rejection and agonising death, taking their failure and sin upon Himself. Everything Jesus did promoted the dignity, destiny, and restoration of His disciples. He didn't lord over them; on the contrary, He removed limits and gave them His authority.

Jesus *empowered* His disciples. He took a motley bunch of fishermen, tax collectors, and ordinary people, far from the top rungs in society, and made them world changers. Jesus taught and empowered them by the Holy Spirit to perform miracles. He brought them into His glory, and we still know their names.

Jesus promised they'd do even greater things. His desire was not to look like a superstar with adoring fans. Instead, his heart was and is to bring us into the supernatural power and victory He died for, allowing us to soar far beyond our natural abilities.

When leadership and authority are used for self-serving purposes, it's not Kingdom. A great leader helps others fulfil their potential. And greatness in leadership isn't limited to vocation or ministry; it's greatness in your family life, spiritual life, emotional life, relationships, and finances. Love-driven leadership draws us. We may, at times, feel restricted, but when we know the motive behind it is love and our good, it doesn't bring the hurt and mistrust of mishandled authority.

I'm blessed with a husband who's an example of Godly Kingdom leadership. He genuinely wants me to realise my dreams and fulfil my destiny in God. He pours out his time, knowledge, and finances to empower me to rise. He encourages me when I feel inadequate and brings his strength and resources to help me reach greater heights than I could on my own. That's the empowerment side of the coin.

There are also times when he tells me he thinks I'm getting off track. He's not afraid to challenge me when he feels I'm operating out of fear rather than faith. When our children were young, he'd occasionally re-focus me because I tended to people-please and have wrong priorities. That's the protection side of the coin. It wasn't fun, and sometimes I argued and sulked, but over time, I came to value his wisdom and ability to see and help me address my blind spots.

FREE WILL

One characteristic of the Kingdom I can't stress enough is *free will*. Free will is the freedom to choose. From the beginning, God allowed humanity to select its path. Without question, there are consequences for our choices, but we have the right to choose. Have you noticed that when you feel like you don't have a choice in something, it brings inner turmoil? God has given you an internal warning system to help you recognise when something is outside His ways.

God placed two trees in the garden of Eden and gave Adam and Eve the ability to make a wrong choice. There were consequences, but God's love didn't waver. He came looking for them, and when He uncovered what they'd done, He made a way for it to be put right. He made coverings for them and set in motion a plan of restoration formulated before time began.

The word 'submission' means to voluntarily place yourself under the authority of a particular leader or person.[4] No one can demand it of you, and God will not force or coerce you to surrender your will or power. God's way is an invitation to something greater, driven by love. It's easy to mistake bowing to intimidation for Godly submission. The two can look the same outwardly, but one is motivated by fear and self-protection, the other by love and faith. One is pleasing to God; the other is not. It comes down to the motives of our hearts, and sometimes we're not consciously aware of them. If you don't feel emotionally or physically safe to be your authentic self, set appropriate boundaries, or speak truthfully from your heart, you're not living in freedom.

> "Now, the "Lord" I'm referring to is the Holy Spirit, and wherever he is Lord, there is freedom." (2 Corinthians 3:17 TPT)

Remember that the main characteristic of the Kingdom of God is love. Everything must be filtered through that. The Kingdom of darkness is fear-driven. When you're trying to discern between oppression and Kingdom authority, consider whether fear drives your decisions. There were many times I thought I pleased God with my choices to submit to authority only to realise down the track that I was coming under fear.

WHEN THE SNAKE IS IN CHARGE

The serpent used deception to entice Eve away from trusting God. He sowed seeds of doubt in Eve's mind about the goodness of God. He posed a question as to whether God was withholding something good from her and asserted the tree's fruit would make her like God (Genesis 3:5). The thing is, she was already like God. She was created in the His image and carried authority and significance as a daughter of God. She was tempted to take something that God had already freely bestowed. The real fruit of this tree was religion, fear, and oppression. It brought shame, not honour, and stole her authority—creating disconnection with God.

Eve's choice unleashed consequences for all of humanity. Under God's authority, they enjoyed freedom and, through His delegated authority, ruled and reigned with Him. In Satan's Kingdom, they were oppressed through slavery, forfeiting their authority. Humankind chose the way of religion, where rules and structure replace an intimate relationship with God. I'll keep saying it—religion is a counterfeit to God's Kingdom. Knowing right and wrong replaces living in constant connection and communion with Father God.

In chapter two, we'll explore the counterfeit in greater detail and expose its influence and power in our daily lives.

Prayer

Father, thank you for taking me on this journey to freedom. Reveal how the tree of the knowledge of good and evil affects me. Give me eyes to see any untrue beliefs about Kingdom authority so I can walk in the freedom you intend for me. Father, You said you would give me the desires of my heart. I desire truth in my inward parts. Thank you for taking me from strength to strength and glory to glory.
I say "yes" to all you have for me.
In Jesus' Name. Amen.

CHAPTER TWO

Religion Kills

Religion is a killer. God warned Adam and Eve that eating from the tree of the knowledge of good and evil would kill them. Religion was hell-bent on murdering Jesus. The religious leaders of His day cried out "crucify Him" when Pilate wanted to release Him. The spirit of religion attempts to choke God's life out of us and replace it with systems, formulas, and rules. The enemy is still trying to convince us to operate from *knowledge* rather than the Spirit of Christ within us. The religious spirit is a spirit of anti-Christ. In the same way that a python slowly kills its prey, religion methodically crushes the life out of believers.

We live in a world that glorifies busyness with 'crazy busy' as its catchcry. Busyness tempts us to fall back on what we *know* instead of living connected with God. While writing this book, I started to reduce my time seeking the Holy Spirit's guidance and instead wrote from my knowledge of the subjects. It's unlike me, but the overwhelming feeling of having too much to do and too little time created the perfect scenario for me to fall into the busy trap.

Another ploy of religion is to tell us we must die. I believe the misinterpretation of what it means to 'die to self' wreaks havoc on many believers. God indeed said that the wages of sin is death, but Jesus died on our behalf so we could have *abundant life* (John 10:10). I've counselled many Christians trying to put themselves to death. One client wept as she confessed, "I always felt like God wanted to kill me". When there's an overemphasis on dying to self, coupled with the implication that God can't look at us because of our sin, it leaves people feeling that they're unacceptable to God. This can be highly detrimental to mental health and cause Christians to disconnect from their true identity in an attempt to die to self.

When you deny who you are in Christ, it undermines your ability to trust your judgment and can affect your ability to function well. Distrusting your desires, thoughts, and emotions can leave you paralysed and indecisive. You're a new creation in Christ, and His Spirit lives within you. Holy Spirit leads you by pulling you toward God, His truth and your calling. If you constantly doubt what you're feeling, thinking, and sensing, you lose your capacity to be led by God and rely on others to tell you what God wants for your life.

The tree of knowledge of good and evil screams that we are bad, and God is good. The logic follows that we have to die and empty ourselves so that only Christ lives in us. While this sounds 'Christian', and we are to surrender our will to God and invite the Holy Spirit to dwell in and guide us, twisting these truths leads to death, not life. I once heard Bill

Johnson from Bethel Church say, "So many Christians are trying to put to death the resurrected man." There was an 'old man', but we have been crucified with Christ and raised to new life.

> "Since, then, you have been raised with Christ, set your hearts on things above, where Christ is, seated at the right hand of God. Set your minds on things above, not on earthly things. For you died, and your life is now hidden with Christ in God. When Christ, who is your life, appears, then you also will appear with him in glory.
>
> Put to death, therefore, whatever belongs to your earthly nature: sexual immorality, impurity, lust, evil desires, and greed, which is idolatry. Because of these, the wrath of God is coming. You used to walk in these ways, in the life you once lived. But now you must also rid yourselves of all such things as these: anger, rage, malice, slander, and filthy language from your lips." (Colossians 3:1-8 NIV)

We don't put ourselves to death; we put to death our sinful behaviours. God makes a distinction between His children and their behaviour. He won't reject you; He delights in you as His child. You bring Him joy!

THE ACCUSER OF HUMANITY

The stark contrast between God's kingdom and religion was demonstrated when the Scribes and Pharisees presented Jesus with the woman caught in adultery.

"As he was speaking, the teachers of religious law and the Pharisees brought a woman who had been caught in the act of adultery. They put her in front of the crowd.

"Teacher," they said to Jesus, "this woman was caught in the act of adultery. The law of Moses says to stone her. What do you say?"

They were trying to trap him into saying something they could use against him, but Jesus stooped down and wrote in the dust with his finger. They kept demanding an answer, so he stood up again and said, "All right, but let the one who has never sinned throw the first stone!" Then he stooped down again and wrote in the dust.

When the accusers heard this, they slipped away one by one, beginning with the oldest, until only Jesus was left in the middle of the crowd with the woman. Then Jesus stood up again and said to the woman, "Where are your accusers? Didn't even one of them condemn you?"

"No, Lord," she said.

And Jesus said, "Neither do I. Go and sin no more." (John 8:3-11 NLT)

Religion accuses, shames, and focuses on sin. Can you imagine the shame this woman felt being exposed so publicly? The Pharisees weren't interested in her as a person, only that she'd sinned. Everything and everyone was viewed through right and wrong, good and bad. But Jesus didn't judge her. He protected her. How wonderful it must have been for her to realise Jesus was not against her but was her advocate. Jesus found a way, without violating the law, to show mercy and grace. He revealed Himself not as a courtroom judge but as a protector. He modelled the true essence of a loving Father who doesn't encourage or dismiss sin but removes our disgrace and restores our dignity.

The battle between the two kingdoms is evident in the interaction between Jesus and the religious leaders. For years I was perplexed about why He was so compassionate towards sinners yet scathing in his dealings with Scribes and Pharisees.

> "You are nothing but snakes in the grass, the offspring of poisonous vipers! How will you escape the judgment of hell if you refuse to turn in repentance?"
>
> (Matthew 23:33 TPT)

> "Then Jesus addressed both the crowds and his disciples and said, "The religious scholars and the Pharisees sit in Moses' seat as the authorised interpreters of the Law. So listen and follow what they teach, but don't do what they do, for they tell you one thing and do another. They tie on your backs an oppressive burden of religious obligations and insist that you carry them but will never lift a finger to help ease your load. Everything they do is done for show and to be noticed by others. They want to be seen as holy, so they wear oversized prayer boxes on their arms and foreheads with Scriptures inside, and

wear extra-long tassels on their outer garments. They crave the seats of highest honour at banquets and in their meeting places. And how they love to be admired by men with their titles of respect, aspiring to be recognised in public and have others call them 'Reverend.'

"But you are to be different from that. You are not to be called 'master,' for you have only one Master, and you are all brothers and sisters. And you are not to be addressed as 'father,' for you have one Father, who is in heaven. Nor are you to be addressed as 'teacher,' for you have one Teacher, the Anointed One. The greatest among you will be the one who always serves others. Remember this: If you have a lofty opinion of yourself and seek to be honoured, you will be humbled. But if you have a modest opinion of yourself and choose to humble yourself, you will be honoured."

(Matthew 23:1-12 TPT)

Jesus exposed leadership anchored in the counterfeit. The heavy burdens placed on people by their leaders brought death, not life. They misrepresented God and put the Jews in bondage instead of leading them into freedom.

When His disciples suggested operating in judgment and condemnation, Jesus corrected them sharply and exposed the spirit in operation.

And when His disciples James and John saw this, they said, "Lord, do You want us to command fire to come down from heaven and consume them, just as Elijah did?"

But He turned and rebuked them, and said, **"You do not know what manner of spirit you are of.** For the Son of Man did not come to destroy men's lives but to save them." And they went to another village. (Luke 9:55 NKJV)

Satan comes as an angel of light. He may look good, but all he brings is slavery and death. We must be shrewd to escape the snare of religion. The Israelite's season of bondage in Egypt is a picture of the church under the oppression of the religious spirit. It's a spiritual principality that transcends denominations, and we must be alert to its influence. In my early years as a Christian, I judged certain denominations for being affected by religion but failed to recognise how much I was personally affected. It may present differently in different settings, but we're all susceptible to its workings. It's subtle and largely unrecognised because much of it appears as the 'good' side of the tree of the knowledge of good and evil. It's not something to fear, but we should ask God to reveal any ways we've been influenced by religion.

As I look back on the first ten to fifteen years of my Christian walk, I can see just how much I was under religion's influence. Even the way I parented my children was from a religious mindset. There's no shame or condemnation in recognising we've been affected; I don't think there are many Christians who haven't come under it somehow. The blood of Jesus sets us free from all guilt and shame, so let's be willing to see the truth and let go of some of the structures and practices we've clung to that made us feel safe. They're usually not bad or wrong, but if they're more important to us than our living relationship with God, they need to be challenged.

The tree of the knowledge of good and evil exalts knowledge, information, and intellect. It sounds good in theory but lacks the power of the true Gospel to bring freedom and transformation. When we're under the influence of religion, our Christianity is slowly reduced to head knowledge and performance. We know right and wrong, what's expected of us, and we stick to the rules – or try! Without an emotional, experiential connection with God, we go through the motions and miss out on the abundant life Jesus promised.

Religion killed the freedom, innocence, and childlike nature of Adam and Eve's relationship with the Father. Before the Fall, Adam and Eve were naked and felt no shame. They had nothing to hide; they were perfectly at peace and enjoyed intimacy with God. But, after the Fall, shame entered, and they hid from their loving Father.

LIVING IN EGYPT

For 430 years, the Children of Israel were in bondage to the Egyptians. This period of slavery and captivity is a picture of life under Satan's rule. Once more, we see the serpent feature when Moses is tasked with bringing God's people out from under the yoke of slavery. Moses instructs Aaron to throw down his staff, and it turns into a snake as a sign to Pharoah that God sent him. But then, Pharoah calls for his sorcerers. They throw down their staffs, which, likewise, become serpents. The enemy has no originality; he can only copy and counterfeit the moves of

God. God is always victorious, and Aaron's serpent swallows the counterfeit snakes.

Let's look at how the Israelites ended up as slaves in the first place. I find it fascinating that they initially had favour with the Egyptians. Joseph was a great ruler, second only to Pharoah. He brought his family to Egypt during a famine, and there they prospered for generations. It wasn't until years after Joseph's death that things started to change. Seeing their vast numbers and fearing they might side with Egypt's enemies, a new Pharoah decided to enslave them.

> "Now there arose a new king over Egypt, who did not know Joseph. And he said to his people, "Look, the people of the children of Israel are more and mightier than we; come, let us deal shrewdly with them, lest they multiply, and it happen, in the event of war, that they also join our enemies and fight against us, and so go up out of the land." Therefore they set taskmasters over them to afflict them with their burdens. And they built for Pharaoh supply cities, Pithom and Raamses. But the more they afflicted them, the more they multiplied and grew. And they were in dread of the children of Israel. So the Egyptians made the children of Israel **serve with rigour**. And they made their lives bitter with hard bondage—in mortar, in brick, and in all manner of service in the field. All their service in which they made them serve was with rigour." (Exodus 1:8-14 NKJV)

Pharoah schemed to subdue the Children of Israel by oppressing them. In Hebrew, the word "oppress" means; "to be busied with, to become low, to become depressed, be downcast, to be afflicted, to be humiliated, to be weakened."[1] The Israelites lived as slaves for centuries. Slavery became their normal. The Israelites who were alive when it was God's time to bring them out of Egypt had generations of enslaved people in their ancestry. Oppression shaped their individual and collective thought processes. When we're not free to determine our destiny, feelings of powerlessness and hopelessness quickly lead to depression.

Contrast this with when the Israelites first came to Egypt. God placed Joseph in a position of influence, releasing prestige and favour over the entire family.

LIFE IN EGYPT

Pharoah's strategy to control the Israelites was to work them to death. They were so busy they had no time or energy to revolt. They were so exhausted building someone else's empire had no time for God. The Egyptians ensured that the Israelites used their strength to build for them, with no time or energy to create prosperity for themselves.

Picture the Egyptian taskmasters with their whips out, driving the Israelites harder and harder. If they stepped out of line, their captors beat them mercilessly. The Egyptians weren't concerned with the wellbeing of God's children; there was no rest, and only death brought relief.

SLAVES TO RELIGION

The plight of the Israelites is a vivid picture of how Satan uses religion to control Christians. The relational aspect of Christianity is diminished, with rules and regulations taking precedence. The focus is on outward performance and promotes a belief that God is primarily interested in what we do and how we behave. It's often accompanied by a picture of God as a courtroom judge who evaluates and either approves or condemns our performance. When we believe our righteousness and favour with God are tied to performance, we face mission impossible. No matter how much we do or achieve, it's never enough. Jesus becomes our taskmaster, whip in hand, while the Father looks on disapprovingly and, in the end, finds us wanting.

I've counselled countless Christians who were exhausted to the point of burnout by their Christian service. And yet, they still believed they were falling short of God's expectations. I remember sitting with a church leader as she wept, admitting she was concerned for her salvation. When pressed, she confessed her fear that she'd failed God because she'd not led anyone to Christ. There was no joy in her relationship with God, just an overwhelming sense of not measuring up.

The religious spirit makes us feel there are never enough hours in the day. As a result, we neglect ourselves and forfeit our wellbeing to serve God and others. I've watched marriages fail, children estranged, and finances decline due to a slavery mentality in authentic but oppressed Christians. Let me be clear: serving God is wonderful, **but** it becomes oppressive when you work to gain His approval for fear of rejection. Satan uses this lie to keep you busy working *for* God so that you don't spend time *with* God. The enemy knows it's time in prayer, worship, and soaking in God's presence that changes us into His likeness.

FREEDOM OF CHOICE

Slavery removes free will. Enslaved people don't get to make choices about their lives; they're told what they can and can't do. They matter only as long as they spend their lives in the service of their master. Satan wants you to believe God is this kind of master, and one of his favourite tricks is to overemphasise scriptures about laying down your life and surrendering to God to the point that you'll think it's wrong to have any personal desires or dreams.

This thinking leaves many Christians paralysed in their decision-making. They fear making a wrong choice, believing God will punish them. That's no way to live. I rejoice I have a heavenly Father who knows me intimately, knows the future, and knows how things will work out. I feel so blessed to ask my Father for His wisdom in my decision-making, knowing He loves me and will never condemn me (Romans 8:1). The choice is simple; we live from fear or love.

Your Heavenly Father wants you to live a blessed life. His plans for you are good, to give you a hope and a future (Jeremiah29:11). As a loving Father, He leads and guides in directions for your good, though it may not feel like it at the time. He does it because He loves you and knows how He made you, not because you're wrong for wanting to make a different decision—viewing life through a lens of love rather than fear will help you understand God's heart in His voice and word.

Oppression is in operation anytime we don't feel free to make decisions for fear of the consequences. Our God is a God of freedom! Where the Spirit of the Lord is, there is liberty (2 Corinthians 3:17). Our Father wants to parent us into mature sons and daughters, not slaves.

A WAY OF ESCAPE

Our good Father has made a way of escape. Just as He did for the Israelites, God provides a safe passage out of Egypt into the land of promise.

> "Therefore say to the children of Israel: 'I am the Lord; I will bring you out from under the burdens of the Egyptians, I will rescue you from their bondage, and I will redeem you with an outstretched arm and with great judgments. I will take you as My people, and I will be your God. Then you shall know that I am the Lord your God who brings you out from under the burdens of the Egyptians. And I will bring you into the land which I swore to give to Abraham, Isaac, and Jacob; and I will give it to you as a heritage: I am the Lord.'" Exodus 6:6-8 NKJV

The first step is to recognise oppression as distinct from true Kingdom authority.

OPPRESSION IMPACTS OUR IDENTITY

Even after the Israelites escaped the clutches of the Egyptians, they believed themselves weak. Nowhere is it more evident than when they came to enter the Promised Land. On seeing what they perceived as giants in the land, they declared themselves grasshoppers. They *expected* defeat instead of victory. In short, the abuse of the past trained and conditioned them to expect pain and suffering.

It happens to us too. If you suffered abuse and neglect in childhood or adult relationships, it changes how you view yourself. You may assume your mistreatment is because you lack value and worth. You may have believed the harsh words spoken over and to you. But I'm here to tell you the opposite is true. You've been targeted *because* of your value and ability to bring the Kingdom of God to Earth. You're a world changer and carry God Himself within you.

The deep sense of shame accompanying abuse and neglect obscures and distorts the view of ourselves and the world around us, but He provides the antidote.

Slavery didn't alter their physical strength or numbers, but it changed the Israelite's self-perception. Abuse and oppression send the message that we're powerless. The Egyptians, who were actually afraid of their strength, deliberately and systematically beat them down, dehumanising them to the point where they believed the lie.

OPPRESSION IMPACTS OUR VIEW OF GOD

The Israelites struggled with trusting God after Egypt. During the exodus, whenever they encountered resistance, they defaulted to a defeatist position. As crazy as it sounds to us, time and time again, they complained to Moses that they would be better off back in Egypt.

> "And when Pharaoh drew near, the children of Israel lifted their eyes, and behold, the Egyptians marched after them. So they were very afraid, and the children of Israel cried out to the Lord. Then they said to Moses, "Because there were no graves in Egypt, have you taken us away to die in the wilderness? Why have you so dealt with us, to bring us up out of Egypt? Is this not the word that we told you in Egypt, saying, 'Let us alone that we may serve the Egyptians'? For it would have been better for us to serve the Egyptians than that we should die in the wilderness.'" Exodus 14:10-12 NKJV

The Israelites were so familiar with oppressive leadership they couldn't grasp God's goodness. Their lived experience coloured how they saw Moses and, ultimately, God. The familiar becomes normal and a place of 'safety' and comfort even when it's abusive; a case of 'better the devil you know'. The Children of God knew what to expect under the Egyptians, even though it was horrific. Their fear of the unknown was greater than the hell of slavery.

Change is hard. Whether it's a change in our beliefs, relationships, or circumstances, the uncertainty of the new can be overwhelming. We may feel safer remaining in the distress of slavery, but what would happen if we dared embrace something new?

Prayer

Father, help me see Kingdom Authority through the lens of love. Please dissolve the lenses of law and legalism and set me free from deception and oppression. Thank you that I have the mind of Christ and the Holy Spirit so I can discern truth in my innermost being. Father, reveal to me anything hindering me from entering Your rest. In Jesus' Name. Amen.

CHAPTER THREE

Freedom from Shame

Shame is sneaky. It distorts our sense of self and makes it hard to recognise who or what is responsible for our pain. It's like a program running in the background, aiding and abetting oppression. Shame can be described as an overwhelming sense of inadequacy and humiliation. It brings feelings of unworthiness and defectiveness, making us want to hide. Where guilt focuses on our actions, shame focuses on our identity. Guilt says, "I did wrong," but shame says, "I am wrong".

Shame and self-blame go hand in hand. One of the reasons we stay under oppression is we believe mistreatment is our fault. When we think we're the problem, we concentrate on fixing ourselves rather than taking back our authority and addressing the real issue. I once had a client tell me she believed all the bad things that happened to her were because she was bad. The words of an abusive parent travelled with her into adulthood as a core belief. It skewed her sense of who was responsible for the abuse. I've found this to be true for many of the victims of domestic violence.

Another client of mine was in an abusive marriage. She described the outbursts of anger and torrent of abuse from her husband, yet she came to counselling to fix herself. She believed she was the problem. She thought if she could learn to do things just right, the abuse would stop. This scenario is sadly commonplace. My client's shame and her husband's narrative that his anger was her fault left her believing she was to blame. She couldn't see that he was responsible and that his behaviour was reprehensible and unacceptable. Until and unless we confront shame, we'll continue to live in confusion and oppression.

SHAME TO GLORY

Eve's story reveals God's plan to take women from shame to glory. Shame entered the picture at the Fall. When God came looking for Adam and Eve, their response was a dead giveaway to their feelings of deep shame. Their Heavenly Father, who walked with them in the garden, was now someone to fear. They hid because they suddenly knew they were naked. Before the Fall, they were naked and unashamed (Genesis 2:25). Now they felt exposed and judged. Do you ever feel unworthy to stand before Father God? Have you ever felt like you didn't measure up or you've fallen short of God's expectations?

Let's look at it from Eve's perspective. She fell for the serpent's lie, and the consequences were almost beyond comprehension for her and all humanity. Talk about wanting to hide! Imagine having your failure told and retold for eternity. We know that Adam also fell, but we know God saw it all before the foundation of the world and set in motion a plan of redemption. I can only imagine the level of distress, shame, and blame of

Eve's self-talk. I think about mistakes I've made that pale in comparison and the acute embarrassment and humiliation that overwhelmed me.

Shame hides. It may manifest outwardly as embarrassment or extreme shyness, but shame is hiding at the core. For years, I had no idea how shame dictated my emotions, self-esteem, and thought patterns. I'm the youngest of four siblings, and while my parents had a faith in God, they weren't attending church by the time I was born. As a result, my knowledge of God was minimal. Although I attended a Presbyterian school, the church held no interest. However, in my early twenties, my two brothers became Christians, and they introduced me to God. I encountered Jesus while holidaying in Spain but kept my newfound faith quiet because I was scared of the reaction of family and friends.

I had a reputation as the 'party girl'. I was a binge drinker and prided myself on being able to outdrink most of my friends. I later realised much of my pull toward alcohol was to medicate my extreme shyness, a symptom of shame. As with Adam and Eve, my primary reaction was to hide.

Shyness is how we hide inside ourselves. We stay quiet to avoid exposing ourselves to ridicule because we believe we're inferior. Shame keeps us locked up for fear of judgment, hidden from the world. We may find a few safe people with whom we can be ourselves, but we prefer to remain unseen with new people or in groups. Shyness isn't the same as introversion. Introversion is personality-based, while shyness is shame-based. Introverts get their energy from being alone; they enjoy more one on one social interaction and are usually very self-aware. Shyness, however, can be debilitating, leaving the person inhibited and acutely uncomfortable in social situations, causing them to withdraw.

Social fear was a hallmark of my life before becoming a Christian. Most of my decisions were to avoid fear triggers. I didn't realise it at the time, but I was so bound by shame that hiding was my default. Social situations were challenging, particularly with new people. I had little confidence, believing I had no value to add to any conversation.

Years later, I was a leader at my church, attending an evening service. At the end of the meeting, the guest speaker offered to pray for anyone desiring freedom from shame. I had no intention of responding, but I sensed the Holy Spirit urging me to go forward. It was the last thing I wanted to do. I didn't think I had a shame issue, so I argued with Him.

Eventually, begrudgingly, I went down the front for prayer. It didn't feel like anything happened. But the next day, God exposed my lens of shame. While praying, memories of my sinful life before becoming a Christian flooded my mind as shame and disgrace overtook me. I felt unworthy and stained beyond repair. I then sensed I was standing before my Heavenly Father. He asked me to look at Him. My head was bowed, and I couldn't bear to look up. He persisted, and eventually, I raised my head. As I did, the revelation of what Jesus did for me on the Cross hit home. His blood washed away all the sin, shame, and disgrace. It wasn't hidden from sight; it was removed—permanently.

I felt clean and realised I'd pushed away from the memories because they were shame-filled. I'd cognitively accepted that I was forgiven but was unaware of the shame buried in my heart. We don't have to be aware of shame for it to impact and influence our emotions and behaviour.

THE MEASURING STICK

A typical response to feeling inadequate is trying to be and do everything perfectly. The person covers their perceived internal imperfection with outward performance. Perfectionists hold themselves to an impossibly high internal standard. They judge themselves against their personal measuring stick and never measure up.

The tree of the knowledge of good and evil is one of judgment. When we eat of that tree, we view everything through a lens of good and bad, right, and wrong. Shame brings out the measuring stick, not for behaviour, but *identity*. Eve measured herself and came up short. Where once being naked was natural, it now felt like exposure. If you're eating the fruit of that tree, you'll constantly measure yourself and find yourself wanting. This happens when we navigate from evil to good; love and connection with God are tied to the correct behaviour. The tree of life, or God's way, is the opposite— right behaviour comes from love and connection with God.

LEARNING TO RECEIVE

Adam and Eve made coverings for themselves to hide their nakedness, but that wasn't God's way. God's covering is love, and it looks like Jesus. Our job is to receive the gift He offers, which sounds easy, yet our hearts struggle. I often have clients tell me it feels too good to be true. Life has taught us we have to work for what we're meant to receive. Jesus said that to enter the Kingdom of Heaven, we need to become like children receiving from our Father. Shame tells us we must earn salvation. Good parents don't expect children to earn their love—they love them unconditionally.

As a new Christian, I struggled to receive God's love. I brought the weight of perfectionism into the relationship and worked hard to gain His approval. I was determined to prove to God how much I loved Him, convincing Him of my worth through obedience, blind to the shame driving me into the ground.

I've always been passionate about God's presence and seek places where I can encounter Him in a greater measure. Bethel Church in Redding was one of those places. I visited for a conference in 2010 and returned in 2012. My prayer was for a life-changing encounter with the Lord. I longed to be free from my prison of fear and timidity. I'd read about the likes of Randy Clark and Heidi Baker, whose God encounters marked them forever, and I was hungry for something like that.

We were at a Bethel healing conference, sitting about three rows from the front as Bill Johnson preached. He spoke about how spiritual gifts can be imparted from one person to another, and I was suddenly aware of God's presence. Then, I heard Him say, "Get up out of your seat and stand in front of Bill". Terror gripped my heart, and everything in me screamed, "NO!!!". Creating a spectacle in front of all those people was too much to bear. Bill paused, I froze with fear, and it felt like the world stopped, waiting for me to respond to God.

Bill moved on after a few seconds, and I no longer sensed God's presence. I knew I'd missed an opportunity for the encounter I craved. I was bitterly disappointed in myself and filled with grief. I cried off and on during the rest of our time in Redding.

A friend who came with me bought a CD from Chris Gore and gave it to me. I took it home to Australia and listened a few days later. The teaching centred on receiving God's love, concentrating on the reactions of Peter and John after failing Jesus at His crucifixion. Both apostles deserted Jesus at His arrest (Mark 14:50–5). Peter denied Him three times even though he earnestly desired to be faithful. John, however, was at the crucifixion, while Peter was nowhere to be found. The teaching contrasted the responses of the two men, and in particular, their relationship with Jesus. Peter focused on *his* love for Jesus ("Even if I have to die with You, I will never deny You." Matthew 26:35). But John was more focused on Jesus' love *for him* ("Now there was leaning on Jesus' bosom one of His disciples, whom Jesus loved." John 13:23).

As I listened, God spoke to my heart. He showed me our relationship was heavily focused on my obedience. I felt accepted and loved when I thought I was getting it right. I thought I understood God's grace and unconditional love but walking through failure told a different story. As painful as it was, as I walked through the process of forgiving myself, letting go of self-righteousness and receiving God's unmerited favour, I understood the message of the Gospel in a whole new way.

I realised that, like the elder brother in the prodigal son parable, I believed doing things just right and being a 'good girl' made me worthy of the Father's attention and affection. I now came to the Father like the prodigal. I felt unworthy of His love and had to learn to receive it by faith. It took failure to wake me up to the goodness and kindness of my Father.

SHAME RESOLVED

The antidote to shame isn't performance; it's the blood of Jesus. In the same way that the Father provided fig leaves for Adam and Eve to cover their nakedness, we have a robe of righteousness through Christ. Shame's legacy of nakedness is covered by the extravagant love of Jesus on the Cross. No matter what you've done, haven't done, or what's been done to you, Jesus calls you righteous. You "put on Christ" (Romans 13:14) when you accept His gift of righteousness. It's a glorious exchange. On the Cross, Jesus carried every mistake, every failure, and all our sins. He took every shame and gave righteousness in its place – His perfect record of right standing before the Father. What a gift!

> "And you shall know the truth, and the truth shall make you free." *(*John 8:32 NKJV)

Jesus said that the truth would set us free. Unfortunately, just *knowing* the truth in my mind wasn't enough to set me free. The truth that sets us free is more than an intellectual exercise. When the Bible speaks of ‹knowing' the truth, it refers to an *experiential relationship*. It's easy to get frustrated and discouraged because we understand something cognitively, yet nothing has changed emotionally. The Bible tells us that we believe with our hearts and not just our minds.

> "Then He said to them, "O foolish ones, and slow of heart to believe in all that the prophets have spoken!" (Luke 24:25 NKJV)

> "Then Philip said, "If you believe with all your heart, you may." And he answered and said, "I believe that Jesus Christ is the Son of God." (Acts 8:37 NKJV)

To be set free from shame and embrace the truth of our righteousness, we need to encounter God in the parts of our hearts that hold the shame. Then, we can pray and ask Him to come to those parts that need His healing truth. Jesus carried your sin and shame because He loves you and wants you free. Therefore, he is willing and able to answer your prayers for healing and freedom.

THE EXPECTATION OF GLORY

Shame causes us to hide, but glory has the opposite effect. To be glorified means to be honoured and held in high esteem. When you know in your mind and believe in your heart that you're righteous and worthy of love, you become comfortable before God and people. Jesus brings us into *His* victory and glory.

> Living within you is the Christ who floods you with the expectation of glory! This mystery of Christ, embedded within us, becomes a heavenly treasure chest of hope filled with the riches of glory for his people, and God wants everyone to know it! (Colossians 1:27 TPT)

Think of Queen Esther after she saved her nation, King David after defeating Goliath, or countless others we read about in Scripture. The incredible thing is that Jesus brings us, His church, His bride, His daughters, into His victory and glory. You were made to carry the glory of God and shine for the world to see.

Even after Eve disobeyed, God promised her redemption. He's a good Father whose heart is always for restoration and redemption. It's interesting to note that one of the consequences of the Fall for woman was that her husband would rule (have dominion) over her. It wasn't God's original intention for how a husband and wife would interact; it was a direct result of Eve's choice to embrace the knowledge of good and evil.

God declared that Eve's seed would crush the serpent's head. Even as God addressed Eve's failure, He released the promise of restoration. From Eve's generational line would come the One to overcome the serpent for good. The glory lost because of the Fall would be restored. He didn't leave Eve in shame but revealed His plan to bring all womanhood into glory. Jesus, the seed of Eve, crushed the serpent's head, and Mary brought Him into the world.

Think about Mary for a minute. She was so young and brave. She believed in God for the impossible – to be pregnant with God's Son without ever being with a man. She yielded herself wholly to God's plan, regardless of the personal cost. Mary birthed a miracle but experienced judgment and the real possibility of Joseph divorcing her. She faced shame and condemnation through no fault of her own. She was righteous before God and shunned by the religious self-righteous. And yet, Mary was willing to suffer judgment and shame to obey God.

Mary's whole future was at risk, and yet she trusted God.

> "Gabriel answered, "The Spirit of Holiness will fall upon you, and almighty God will spread his shadow of power over you in a cloud of glory! This is why the child born to you will be holy, and he will be called the Son of God. What's more, your aged aunt, Elizabeth, has also become pregnant with a son. The 'barren one' is now in her sixth month. Not one promise from God is empty of power. Nothing is impossible with God!"
>
> Then Mary responded, saying, "Yes! I will be a mother for the Lord! As his servant, I accept whatever he has for me. May everything you have told me come to pass." And the angel left her." (Luke 1:35-38 TPT)

Mary's obedience heralded the crushing of the serpent's head. She trusted God and, in so doing, *birthed victory for all humanity*. Mary obeyed where Eve fell. God worked with a young woman to break the oppression originating with the Fall. How wonderful is our God! He didn't let the serpent get away with shaming His daughters; instead, his mercy and kindness extended toward womankind to bring us out of shame and oppression into glory and victory. Mary is remembered for her faith and obedience. Her story is celebrated and retold the world over. Her willingness to be shamed before man for the sake of her Father's plan is honoured before man for eternity.

GOD'S NOT DONE WITH YOU

When I was little, if I bumped my head on the table, my dad would sit me on his knee and together, we'd smack the table for hurting me. Dad lovingly protected me; anything that caused me pain was subject to his vengeance – even if it was my fault. This is the heart of our Heavenly Father, who not only took vengeance on the serpent, He sits us on His lap and invites us into His plan, empowering us to bring down the enemy of our souls.

God won't leave you in your shame. No matter what's been done to you or what you've done, it's not the end. God is a liberator and restorer, but He doesn't stop there. Like a protective father who wants to restore His child's dignity, He lends us His strength and glory to execute justice on our oppressor.

God filled Mary with His Spirit, and she became pregnant with the Messiah! She carried Jesus, the Victory of the World, within her. God does the same for you. You're filled with the Holy Spirit, and Christ is being formed in you. You carry victory within you.

The victory is not for you alone; it's for you to share with others. As you birth your triumph and nurture it to maturity, it will set many sons and daughters free. It's time to come out of hiding. It's time to let go of shame and see yourself as you really are. Jesus has removed your garments of shame and given you a robe of righteousness. The Father wants to show off His handiwork. He wants the world to see His wonderful creation – **you**! You carry His image and hold keys to victory for nations.

Let His Spirit arise in you as you step into your God-given identity. The world needs you.

The Father is inviting us to take part in birthing His victory in the world. When you became a believer, Jesus came to live inside you. You carry the victory of the world just as Mary did! Jesus grew and developed in Mary's womb until the day came to birth her victory. What triumph are you carrying that God will use to free others and glorify himself?

God never wanted for you to suffer pain, loss, and disgrace. Whether shame was imprinted through the words and actions of others, or like Eve, your choices left you feeling unworthy; your Heavenly Father will not leave you there. Instead, the Lord will arm you with authority and special grace to take out the enemy in the same area he dared wound you.

BEAUTY FOR ASHES

When we endure abuse, shame can take root at the deepest levels. Isaiah's writings note the effects that abuse, trauma, and sin have on our soul and body.

> "The Spirit of the Sovereign Lord is on me,
> because the Lord has anointed me
> to proclaim good news to the poor.
> He has sent me to bind up the **brokenhearted**,
> to proclaim freedom for the **captives**
> and release from darkness for the **prisoners**,
> to proclaim the year of the Lord's favour
> and the day of vengeance of our God,

to comfort all who **mourn**,
and provide for those who **grieve** in Zion—
to bestow on them a crown of beauty
instead of ashes,
the **oil of joy**
instead of **mourning**,
and a garment of praise
instead of a **spirit of despair**.
They will be called **oaks of righteousness**,
a planting of the Lord
for the display of his splendour.
They will rebuild the ancient ruins
and restore the places long devastated;
they will renew the ruined cities
that have been devastated for generations.
Strangers will shepherd your flocks;
foreigners will work your fields and vineyards.
And you will be called **priests of the Lord**,
you will be named **ministers of our God**.
You will feed on the wealth of nations,
and in their riches you will boast.
**Instead of your shame
you will receive a double portion,
and instead of disgrace
you will rejoice in your inheritance**.
And **so you will inherit a double portion in your land,
and everlasting joy will be yours.**
"For I, the Lord, **love justice**;
I hate robbery and wrongdoing.

> In my faithfulness **I will reward my people**
> and make an **everlasting covenant with them.**
> **Their descendants will be known among the nations**
> **and their offspring among the peoples.**
> **All who see them will acknowledge**
> **that they are a people the Lord has blessed."**
> I delight greatly in the Lord;
> my soul rejoices in my God.
> For he has clothed me with garments of salvation
> and **arrayed me in a robe of his righteousness,**
> as a bridegroom adorns his head like a priest,
> and as a bride adorns herself with her jewels.
> For as the soil makes the sprout come up
> and a garden causes seeds to grow,
> so the Sovereign Lord will make righteousness
> and praise spring up before all nations."
> (Isaiah 61 NIV)

This Scripture is deeply significant for those who have suffered seasons of pain and trauma. Isaiah speaks to the impact of abuse and loss. God doesn't sit outside our pain. He understands the devastation experienced by many of His daughters. The Scripture paints a picture of God's provision for complete restoration and compensation, with a promise of double honour for those who have suffered shame and disgrace. He exchanged His beauty for our ashes, and He offers to trade our defeat for His victory, our shame for His glory. Our part is to let go of our ashes (shame) and receive His beauty (glory).

I didn't understand the significance of beauty and ashes for a long time. What does beauty have to do with anything? Then, as I studied, it made more sense. I discovered that covering your head with ashes was symbolic of self-abhorrence and humiliation. It speaks of shame, worthlessness, distress, and grief, depicting desolation and ruin. The word for 'beauty', on the other hand, is a type of fancy headdress, a bonnet that men of position wore, bridegrooms or priests, a sign of joy, celebration, and honour.

There's an invitation to exchange your shame, dishonour and past ruin for His glory, joy, and honour. But it's a process. One of forgiving others, forgiving ourselves and letting go of our old identity. Shame tells us that if others knew the *real* us, they'd walk away. Healing from shame begins by inviting Jesus to be with us in our painful, shame-filled memories. Shame tells us to hide, but we lock ourselves away from God and people when we do that. God wants to unlock the prison doors and open the hidden places, so He can wash our wounds and give us His righteousness.

INSIGHTS INTO SHAME

I had a dream once that gave me insight into how shame hinders our mental health and healing. I dreamed I gave birth to a baby, but I forgot I had a child after a month. I failed to feed or care for my baby, and it died. I remember the distress vividly. I couldn't believe what I'd done. What woman could forget she had a child? The shame was overwhelming, and my inability to forgive myself was so intense I couldn't face what I'd done. I put the dead baby in a cupboard and shut the door, pretending it never existed. You may imagine how thrilled I was when I woke up and realised it was a dream!

This is how shame works. The humiliation and pain of our perceived deficiencies are so great we can't face them. Jesus wants to exchange it for His righteousness, but he won't force His way into our lives. We must grant Him access to our hearts for His healing and freedom to flow.

It can be hard to let go when we haven't validated our pain and suffering. We're wired for connection, and having someone empathise with us in our pain brings healing. Jesus gives us that. Even if the perpetrator of the abuse never acknowledges our pain, Jesus does. When we hand our ashes to Him, they're in safe hands.

A client of mine suffered greatly at the hands of her father. She held so much anger toward him that although she was a Christian and knew forgiveness was the better path, she struggled to let go of her anger and pain. In one of our sessions, I asked if she was willing to hear what Jesus wanted to tell her about letting go of her hurts. She agreed, and immediately her countenance changed – she gasped and wept uncontrollably. A few minutes passed, and the emotion gradually subsided. Finally, I asked what had happened.

She described a picture of Jesus standing in a large warehouse in Heaven. The warehouse contained all her hurts – all the injustices she suffered. Jesus saw everything, her heart was precious to Him, and all that had happened to her mattered to the Father. The love and acknowledgment of Jesus gave her the courage to forgive her father. She released the anger and pain and allowed Jesus to carry it so her heart could be free.

She contacted me about a month later to tell me she felt wonderfully free emotionally and spiritually. She knew she had finally and fully forgiven her father.

We can't experience the fullness and freedom of new life in Christ until we choose to let go. When we forgive ourselves and others, we're open to receiving His glory in place of our shame. Are you ready for the exchange? Are you willing to let go of the humiliation, shame, anger, pain, false identity, and fear? It's not easy, but you're not alone. God will walk with you in the process.

LETTING GO OF THE DEBT

When Jesus teaches about forgiveness in the book of Matthew, He puts it in terms of monetary debt. His parable helped me understand what happens in our hearts when we forgive. Think of the offences and mistreatment that occur in terms of property. If I take your car for a drive and crash it, you're left with a damaged car. Forgiving releases the debt of the damage, and it's the Cross that makes it just and fair.

Forgiving ourselves is often more difficult than releasing the offences of others. Yet, healing from shame and learning to forgive ourselves go hand in hand. Letting the regret, guilt, and shame for the things we have done flow from our hearts to the Cross brings freedom. Let go of the judgment you've held against yourself and allow the blood of Jesus to dissolve the shame.

Jesus came to heal the brokenhearted and set the captives free. The price Jesus paid gains us not only entry into eternal life, it also purchased our healing and complete restoration. But to embrace our new identity, we have first to let go of the old.

It may be helpful to schedule a specific time to sit with God and ask Him to show you any hidden shame. As you wait on the Lord, memories may surface along with feelings of shame and inadequacy. As this happens, ask Jesus to help you release it at the Cross. Ask for the truth to replace the lies and for the lens of good and evil to be removed. Use the prayer at the end of the chapter to help guide you. Scheduling an appointment with a Christian counsellor or inner healing ministry may fast track the process and help you overcome any blockages to freedom.

As shame melts away, focus on the victory growing within you, allow yourself to dream about what it looks like for you. You're a new creation, a daughter of God. You are His masterpiece, and He desires to put you on display. He created you perfectly in every way, and he delights in you. The glory you carry is not just about what you do, but who you are—His glory is infused in your DNA because you are in Him, and He is in you.

Prayer

Father, thank you that I'm fearfully and wonderfully made. I renounce the lie that something is wrong with me, and I receive the truth that you created me perfectly. I forgive those whose actions have left me feeling shameful and unworthy. I choose to let go of any judgment I've held against myself, and I embrace the truth that I am righteous and holy before You. Thank you for exchanging my shame for Your glory. Please open my eyes to the seeds of life You've placed within me and help me see the victory you have called me to bring forth. In Jesus' Name, Amen.

CHAPTER FOUR

Freedom from Control

> "Jesus said to the people who believed in him, "You are truly my disciples if you remain faithful to my teachings. And you will know the truth, and the truth will set you free." (John 8:31-32 NLT)

Jesus declared that truth frees us. If that's so, then it follows that deception keeps us in bondage. If you think about it, it makes sense as I'm sure none of us would willingly remain in bondage if we understood that's not where God wants us. Genesis says that the serpent was the most cunning of all creatures (Genesis 3:1). He looks for weaknesses and uses subtle strategies to entice us to react in the way he wants. Our victory lies in recognising his tactics and discerning between truth and error. We see Jesus contend with Satan a few times in Scripture, and His responses are rich with wisdom and insight.

JESUS OVERCOMES THE SPIRIT OF CONTROL

> "After his baptism, as Jesus came up out of the water, the heavens were opened, and he saw the Spirit of God descending like a dove and settling on him. And a voice from heaven said, "This is my dearly loved Son, who brings me great joy." Then Jesus was led by the Spirit into the wilderness to be tempted there by the devil. For forty days and forty nights he fasted and became very hungry." (Matthew 3:16-17, Matthew 4:1-2 NLT)

Shortly after the Father publicly declared His sonship, Jesus faced Satan in the wilderness. The temptations of the enemy focused on His identity. Satan repeatedly asked Jesus to prove Himself to be the Son of God by doing what he, Satan, told Him to do. In other words, Satan was trying to use His identity to control Him. He insinuated that if Jesus were the Son of God, He would behave in a particular way—the enemy's way. Can you see how crafty he is?

We see the same scenario in Luke 4, but this time it's subtler. Here Jesus makes a public declaration about His identity. Again, He's challenged by Satan, but the challenge comes through people. In the first instance, the Father declares, and Satan challenges Jesus directly. In the second situation, Jesus makes the declaration and is challenged by people.

We all face two challenges to our identity. The first happens after hearing the Father's decree about who we are, coming as a direct assault on our minds. The second comes once we've embraced what the Father says about us, and we step into our identity, declaring it to the world.

"When he came to Nazareth, where he had grown up, he went into the synagogue, as he always did on the Sabbath. When Jesus came to the front to read the Scriptures, he was handed the scroll of the prophet Isaiah. He unrolled the scroll and found where it is written, "The Spirit of the Lord is upon me, and he has anointed me to be hope for the poor, healing for the brokenhearted, and new eyes for the blind, and to preach to prisoners, 'You are set free!' I have come to share the message of Jubilee, for the time of God's great acceptance has begun." After he read this he rolled up the scroll, handed it back to the attendant, and sat down. Everyone stared at Jesus, wondering what he was about to say. Then he added, "Today, these Scriptures came true in front of you."

Everyone was impressed by how well Jesus spoke, in awe of the beautiful words of grace that came from his lips. But they said among themselves, "Who does he think he is? Isn't he Joseph's son, who grew up here in Nazareth?"

Jesus said to them, "I suppose you'll quote me the proverb, 'Doctor, go and heal yourself before you try to heal others.' And you'll say, 'Work the miracles here in your hometown that we heard you did in Capernaum.' But let me tell you, no prophet is welcomed or honored in his own hometown.

"Isn't it true that many widows lived in the land of Israel during the days of the prophet Elijah when he locked up the heavens for three and a half years and brought a devastating famine over all the land? But he wasn't sent to any of the widows living in that region. Instead, he was sent to a foreign place, to a widow in Zarephath of Sidon. Or have you not considered that the prophet Elisha healed only Naaman, the Syrian, rather than one of the many Jewish lepers living in the land?"

When everyone present heard Jesus' words, they erupted with furious rage. They mobbed Jesus and threw him out of the city, dragging him to the edge of the cliff on the hill on which the city had been built, ready to hurl him off. But he walked right through the crowd, leaving them all stunned." (Luke 4:16-29 TPT)

Jesus declares himself the fulfilment of Isaiah's prophecy, agreeing with His God-given identity. He then refuses to prove himself to the crowd, focusing on His mission—to do what He sees the Father doing. He didn't deviate from that.

One of the primary ways Satan attempts to control God's people is to come with the subtle accusation, "If you were *really* a Christian, you would…". You can fill in the blanks, but the list is endless.

"You would read the Bible more."
"You would pray more."
"You would do more at Church."
"You would help that person."
"You would be a better daughter."

These thoughts can come directly into your mind or through others, but the result is the same. They become drivers to get you to concentrate on improving your performance. It's not an issue of whether behaviours are good or bad; the directive comes from Satan, not the Father. It's one of the reasons we get caught up in busyness and burnout; we believe it's God behind us with the whip. Anytime we feel compelled to perform a good work to prove our identity as a son or daughter of God, it's not from the Father. The Father declares we are His, based on relationship and covenant, not performance.

Anytime you feel the need to prove yourself to someone by your good works, you're responding to something other than the voice of God. Sometimes people will knowingly and deliberately use your desire to be faithful to God as a means of control. They send messages that if you were who you say you are, you would do what they want.

Do you notice how Jesus sensed the people's demand for miracles, even though it wasn't spoken directly to Him? He felt the pull in the atmosphere. Something was happening in the spiritual realm, and He knew it. We need to get good at discerning when the enemy attempts to influence us through others. Our war isn't with flesh and blood, and there are times when spiritual forces amplify the impact of people, their words, or actions.

Have you ever sensed the pull from people even though they spoke no words? Even without someone asking outright, you feel the expectation. I vividly remember visiting a lady from my church who was ill. She'd sent me messages the evening prior asking me to come and sit with her because she was unwell. This was someone I often helped, though I'd learned to say no to some of her requests because of family and other commitments.

When I arrived, she was in bed, and another lady from the church was with her. She proceeded to tell me how wonderful her friend had been. She'd come the night before, cooked dinner, and stayed over. Her words were like a dagger in my heart. Guilt and shame reared up, and I felt like I didn't measure up as a Christian. The message my heart heard was, "If you were a good Christian, you would have done that for me." When I left, I sat in the car for a while, processing events. When I decided not to visit the night before, it felt like the right thing to do for my family. Why did I feel so bad when she hadn't been angry or said anything to guilt or shame me?

Sometimes things in the spiritual realm ride in on people's words. When our emotional reaction outweighs what's said, it's either because there's a spiritual dynamic to it or an unhealed emotional wound is being poked. Either way, we can choose not to partner with the lie. Sitting in the car, I recognised I felt guilty because I was partnering with the lie that "I'm not a good Christian". I broke agreement with the lie, and the guilt drained away.

Back to Jesus in Nazareth. A religious spirit tempted Him to satisfy people's demands to gain approval. But, just as Satan tempted Jesus in the desert, it was about proving and validating His identity through works.

> "Then the tempter came to him and said, "How can you possibly be the Son of God and go hungry? Just command these stones to be turned into loaves of bread."
> (Matthew 4:3 TPT)

Significantly, this scene takes place in Jesus' hometown. We often want approval from those we know, particularly those we grew up with. The enemy tries to work through those we love and care for because they're the ones from whom we most desire approval. We then become trapped by our desire for their acceptance and validation.

Jesus had a choice to do what the Father was telling Him and potentially lose people's approval, or give in and do what they (and the enemy) demanded. If He didn't perform miracles, they might conclude He wasn't Messiah. Jesus sensed what was happening in the spiritual realm and called it out while staying true to His mission. Just as Elisha and Elijah only performed miracles for those to whom they were sent, Jesus only responded to the Father. He rejects the manipulation, declaring, "Assuredly I say to you, no prophet is accepted in his own country." (Luke 4:24) He's ok with the crowd's disapproval; His identity and worth are found in yielding to God's Kingdom authority. He remained free to focus on what the Father asked of Him, staying in rest. Had He engaged with proving himself through performance, He would have subjected Himself to Satan's plan. It's a covert form of control that often flies under the radar in our own lives. And if this form of control fails, a more overt attack usually comes into play.

When Jesus refused to bow to the enemy's plans, Satan moved from manipulation to intimidation. He influenced the people to threaten and even kill Jesus by throwing Him off a cliff. But the enemy has no authority over the lives of those who belong to the Father. Despite the efforts of the mob, Jesus passed through the midst of them – demonstrating divine protection. It was not His time to die, and the enemy was rendered powerless in his attempt to steal, kill, and destroy. Jesus entrusted His life to the Father and refused to protect himself by placating the devil.

When you stand against this spirit and refuse its demands, don't be surprised if things heat up for a while. There often comes testing that reveals our level of trust in the Father. How much power do we believe the devil has to harm us? Who are we ultimately going to serve? When we face testing and trials, we discover our level of faith and trust.

Illegitimate means of control tend to fall into three categories; *manipulation*, *intimidation*, or *domination*. Manipulation is subtle and uses a person's *desires* as a means of control. It promises the fulfilment of a desire when we participate in a particular behaviour. Intimidation operates through the victim's *fears*, threatening loss or harm unless a specific behaviour is adopted. Finally, domination is when a person physically overpowers another.

MANIPULATION

Manipulation is *"a means to influence or control someone to your advantage, without anyone knowing it."* [1]

Rather than openly asking a person to do something and being willing to accept a refusal, manipulation seeks to press someone in a particular direction in an underhanded way. Manipulation says, "if you do what I want, I'll give you what you want." Manipulation takes your desires and turns them against you. They may even use Godly desires to control you. Our most significant exposure areas usually stem from morally upright and pure desires.

After becoming a Christian, I realised I wanted to help struggling people. While it was a noble desire, it sometimes left me open to manipulation. Some people sense it in you and know how to push your buttons! I remember one lady saying to me, "Christians never really help you; they just say they'll pray for you but never do anything practical to show they care."

It hit me, like a ton of bricks, and a voice inside said, "I'll show you what a *real* Christian is like!" I set myself up for manipulation and found it impossible to say no to all requests. For a season, I was controlled by her demands. Her words played into my desire to be a good Christian and care for people, whether intentional or not.

It's easy to find ourselves busy doing lots of seemingly good things for God while missing the things He's given us responsibility for. If we can't say no to people's demands, we lose control and allow the priorities of others to dictate our lives. We leave ourselves open to manipulation and control when we don't set proper boundaries.

I get sad when I see Christian marriages deteriorate because of the couple's inability to say no to people pulling on them. We're first responsible for our wellbeing, which includes our relationship with God, physical health, rest and so on. Finding the balance of caring for ourselves, our relationships, work, and ministry isn't always straightforward, but it begins with learning to say no.

If we struggle to say no, establish healthy boundaries, or find ourselves resenting the demands on us, there is freedom available. But it requires a shift. We must move from tying our beliefs about ourselves and our performance from people to God. It doesn't mean we never listen to people's perspectives; we weigh their words, consider our needs, and ask God for His perspective. Empowerment comes when we resolve the underlying lies we believe about ourselves.

Manipulation tends to focus on the desires not surrendered to God, weaponising them against us. In the same way, The enemy used Eve's desire for wisdom and Godlikeness to lure her away from the Father. Any desire that's not surrendered to God can be used to control us. Therefore, all desires, including good and Godly ones, must be held loosely. For example, I've always known I'm called to full-time ministry and have a deep desire to serve God. But left unchecked, that desire saw me controlled by people, including church leaders. If not for my husband's wisdom, persistence, and Holy Spirit hounding me to lay it down, I'm not sure where I would have ended up.

I clearly remember when God asked me to put ministry on the proverbial altar. I knew He'd given it to me but sensed He wanted me to hand it back to Him. I'm sorry to say it was a wrestle! It took days before I wholly surrendered, but a new sense of freedom was released when I did. I was no longer bound by the fear that I'd fail in ministry unless I did everything others wanted. God adjusted my thinking, and I was able to operate from a position of serving Him rather than caving to the demands of people.

Career success is another desire susceptible to manipulation. If I can't surrender my desire to God and trust that all promotion comes from Him, I'll be tempted to say yes to every demand, no matter how unreasonable. Any area of our lives not surrendered to God becomes a weapon in the hand of our enemy to enslave us.

KNOWING THE VOICE OF GOD

We need to get good at distinguishing between the voice of the Father and all other voices if we're to walk in freedom. As we've seen, whenever the drive to do something is to prove our identity, it's a good bet we're being driven by the enemy rather than led by the Spirit.

Accusation and criticism are more weapons in the enemy's arsenal. When authority figures consistently blame us for their abusive behaviour, it trains our ears to expect harsh criticism instead of gentle correction from God. As a result, we accept and live under condemnation and accusation because we mistake their misuse of authority for God's voice.

We can hear that God is loving and believe it's true, but our grid for love is skewed. Basically, we don't know what we don't know. After twenty generations of living in bondage and oppression, the Israelites had no concept of God as a ruler. It's hard to know what to look for if we've not experienced the voice of Kingdom authority.

God's Word gives keys to help us discern the voice of our Heavenly Father. When we know our Father's voice, we'll discern voices bent on our destruction more easily.

THE FATHER'S VOICE DOES NOT ACCUSE.

The Bible calls Satan "the accuser of the brethren" (Revelation 12:10). His accusations may come through the words of others or directly to our minds. Accusations illicit feelings of guilt and leave us feeling we must defend ourselves and our actions. I've found myself lying in bed at night rehearsing responses (justifications) to accusations that were only in my mind. I vividly remember one evening while I was doing this; I sensed God asking, "What are you doing?". I love how His questions shine a spotlight, illuminating things we've not seen till that moment. I hadn't thought about my self-talk or the emotional impact of entertaining these thought processes.

I remember making a decision I was pretty sure a friend of mine wouldn't like. I found myself having an imaginary conversation, explaining why I'd taken that course of action. Then, I felt God pull me up. He showed me that I was defending myself because I felt an accusation coming against me. My friend hadn't said a word, but I could feel it. I'm not sure if it originated in me, the person concerned, or whether it was an assault by the Kingdom of darkness, but the point is that it didn't come from God.

My natural response was to justify the decision to myself. It didn't work because I lay there, carrying on these imaginary conversations and feeling guilty. Finally, God directed me to the passage of Scripture where Jesus faced accusation.

When the Jews brought Jesus before Pilate and Herod, He didn't answer their accusations. He didn't defend Himself or try to convince them of His innocence. In fact, He didn't answer most of their questions. This behaviour was so unusual that the Bible says Pilate was amazed (Matthew 27:11-14, Luke 23:6-9). According to 1 Peter 2:23, Jesus committed Himself to the Father as judge. He didn't answer man's accusations because He belonged to a different Kingdom. He lived His life to please the Father and yielded to Him as the just judge.

We must learn to do the same. When people or Satan bring an accusation against us, we need not defend ourselves. We're yielding to them as the judge if we do— giving their words legitimacy. To follow the example of Jesus is to stand before the Father and commit ourselves to Him as our judge. If we've sinned, then it's before Him that we repent and ask for forgiveness – knowing that the blood of Jesus cleanses us from all unrighteousness. Our sin is lifted, and then we need to forgive ourselves, letting go of guilt and shame.

If we haven't sinned, and the accusation is false, we are to commit ourselves to the Father again. We don't have to convince others of our innocence. We place the matter in the hands of the Father – He is our defender. If and when He chooses, He can make the truth known.

Neil T Anderson once said of self-defence, *"If you are innocent, you don't need a defence, and if you're guilty, you don't have one."*[2]

I realise that these things are much easier said than done. My journey into freedom has been little by little and step by step. As I've recognised my areas of susceptibility and struggle, committing them to God, I've learned how to respond to challenging situations. Many times, I've sought counselling and inner healing to align my heart with my mind. It's one thing to know what to do; it's another thing to have the emotional capacity to do it!

It was for freedom that Christ set us free. So let's make sure we don't allow the enemy to turn our Christianity into a place of slavery. In the next chapter, we'll dive into false guilt; how to recognise it, respond, and gain freedom in Jesus.

Prayer

Father, thank you for giving me the authority to make my own decisions and exercise free will. Would you please reveal any situations where I've surrendered my authority because of manipulation? Father, I ask you to break any unhealthy soul ties with the person or persons. Expose any lies I've agreed with that make me susceptible in this area. Father, would you show me any desires I need to surrender to You? Thank you for setting me free.
In Jesus' Name, Amen.

CHAPTER FIVE

Freedom from Guilt

As a Christian counsellor, I've discovered that feelings of guilt plague many Christians. Guilt disempowers us, leaving us susceptible to relinquishing our authority and open to being controlled by others.

Abuse and religion make it harder for us to connect with our freedom in Christ. Feelings of unworthiness and guilt lead to a sin focus. We get duped into thinking that freedom will come when we address *this* behaviour or do *that* better. Let me assure you; this isn't the answer. Discerning the accuser's voice and choosing not to agree with his lies is the pathway to freedom.

It breaks my heart when people believe the voice of accusation is the voice of God. Discerning between accusation and condemnation are critical to our freedom. Guilt is not a fruit of the Spirit!

> "But the Holy Spirit produces this kind of fruit in our lives: love, joy, peace, patience, kindness, goodness, faithfulness, gentleness, and self-control. There is no law against these things!" (Galatians 5:22-23 NLT)

According to the apostle Paul, the Spirit of God comes with recognisable fruit. The first three are love, joy, and peace. These markers help us discern between God's voice and that of others. The voice of accusation is usually accompanied by guilt and shame, with a side-order of manipulation.

THE TWO GUILTS

There are two types of guilt – one that leads to life and another that produces death. One comes from the Kingdom of God and the other from the Kingdom of darkness. Therefore, your capacity to walk in your God-given authority depends on your discernment of the difference.

> "God designed us to feel remorse over sin in order to produce repentance that leads to victory. This leaves us with no regrets. But the sorrow of the world works death." (2 Corinthians 7:10 TPT)

> "This is the message we have heard from Him and announce to you that God is Light, and in Him, there is no darkness at all. If we say that we have fellowship with Him and yet walk in the darkness, we lie and do not practice the truth; but if we walk in the Light as He Himself is in the Light, we have fellowship with one

another, and the blood of Jesus His Son cleanses us from all sin. If we say that we have no sin, we are deceiving ourselves, and the truth is not in us. If we confess our sins, He is faithful and righteous, so that He will forgive us our sins and cleanse us from all unrighteousness. If we say that we have not sinned, we make Him a liar and His word is not in us." (1 John 1:5-9 NASB)

Once and for all, Jesus resolved our guilt at the Cross. As you acknowledge and repent, you're free and can release your feelings of guilt to the Lord. Remember the parable of the prodigal son? The father ran toward his son without regard for protocol or cultural norms. The father's love was passionate, and he ignored his son's offer to become a servant. Instead, he restored the son to his position of authority and threw a party. We're restored to our full authority when we turn from sin in true repentance. We don't have to work our way back into our Father's 'good books'.

When it comes to the guilt that brings death, I've observed that it's often tied to gaining or maintaining people's approval. In the past, when I believed I didn't measure up to the standards or expectations of others, I felt guilty. It took time, but I've learned to recognise it quickly and free myself.

There was a time when avoiding guilty feelings was my primary motivation for doing things. It was particularly evident at church. I'd get upset when asked to do something, not wanting to, but be desperate to avoid the guilt associated with disappointing people. I felt trapped in a lose-lose situation. I'd usually say yes, but it was out of fear, not love. I wanted to *be* loving and *look* loving, believing that I wasn't a good Christian if I said no to a request. It was a vicious cycle.

I realised I was governed more by people's opinions than God's, causing me to strive for approval. God wants love to be our motivation. He looks at our hearts, longing for our good deeds to come from the overflow of His love for us. In 1 Corinthians 13, Paul tells us that all our good works are meaningless without love. Guilt avoidance is self-focused and fear-based. I realised I needed to do some work on my heart.

When I understood I was influenced more by the Kingdom of darkness than God's Spirit in my good works, it revolutionised my relationship with Him. I'd reacted to guilt like a crack of the whip, moving this way and that to avoid those terrible emotions. I came close to burnout because I wasn't Spirit-led. In the same way that the Egyptians enslaved God's people to subdue them, our enemy keeps us so busy with 'good works' we miss the freedom and authority in being led by the Spirit.

Moments of connection with God brought peace and oneness with Him. The guilt, unworthiness, and performance mentality would melt away, and I saw that the expectations and whip-cracking were not from Him. Instead, he taught me to recognise the fruit of the Spirit – love, joy, and peace – as the hallmarks of His voice. Guilt didn't fit, and I began to recognise it as a hallmark of control.

Freedom comes when we allow God to set our priorities and make it our goal to please Him alone. Then, he'll guide and direct us to care for our families, ministries, and employers. Otherwise, we can be pulled off course by taking on responsibilities that aren't from Him.

It takes time to build our discernment and learn to distinguish between God's voice and that of the accuser. But we're not alone; the Holy Spirit is here to help. Bringing issues and situations to Him allows His light to shine and expose any lies. When you're feeling guilty in an area or doing something to avoid guilty feelings, the first thing you should do is bring it to Him.

For example, say your child wants you to take them to the park, and when you refuse, they say, "If you loved me, you'd take me." It can lead to intense feelings of guilt. We may begin to believe we're not loving enough, and before we know it, we're at the park! Before it gets to that, draw aside with the Father. Bring your guilt before Him and ask Him to show you if you've sinned. If you feel convicted, ask Him for forgiveness and let go of your guilt.

If you don't sense you've sinned, ask Him to reveal the lie you've agreed with. The lies perpetuating guilt are "I'm not a good parent. I don't love my child enough." When you think you know what the lie is, renounce it aloud. "Father, I renounce the lie that I'm not a good parent and don't love my child enough." Then ask Him to reveal the truth to you. "Father, what is the truth?" Declare the truth out loud. "Father, I receive the truth that I'm a good parent and that You're pleased with me."

There's a common misconception that makes it hard to release guilt. It's the belief that self-punishment will lead to better behaviour. In many of my clients, I've identified the fear that there will be nothing to stop them from sinning if they're free from guilt and shame.

It's tempting to beat ourselves up for our failings, believing that somehow it will help us change. But it's the Holy Spirit who empowers us to walk in righteousness. Nothing from the Kingdom of darkness will ever help us be more righteous. When we let go of the guilt and shame, there's an increased capacity to draw near to God and receive from Him. ***It's His presence that transforms us,*** *not our guilt.*

Sometimes we feel guilty because we've not lived up to other people's expectations. When what people think about us is overly important, we'll be more concerned with what they think than what God has to say. When we seek to please people over God, we open ourselves up to control. The Bible says that the fear of man is a trap. It's a trap the Kingdom of darkness uses to minimise our effectiveness in the Kingdom. It also robs us of joy and peace, those things for which Jesus paid the ultimate price.

Many years ago, I felt overwhelmed with guilt and shame after letting a friend down. I was tormented for days until, during my prayer time, I sensed the Father acknowledge my intense guilt.

"Wow, you must have really sinned to be feeling this bad. Did you murder someone?" There was a cheekiness to His voice.
"No, I didn't murder anyone," I responded.
"Well, what was the sin?"

I realised I hadn't sinned; it was that I hadn't fulfilled someone's expectations of me. I also realised that I didn't feel anywhere near as guilty for my actual sins! I knew my priorities were out of kilter. I was more troubled by letting people down than I was for sinning. I'd fallen into the fear of man. I repented and sensed the Father encouraging me to bring every situation to Him *first* so He could shine His light and show me the truth. If I sinned, I'd repent, ask for forgiveness, and walk free from the guilt. If I hadn't, I'd let go of having to meet people's expectations and be content with knowing God approves of me.

It's been incredibly freeing. I lived with anxiety for many years because I was worried about what others thought of me. I feared their judgment and disapproval. We can be yoked with others' expectations or yoked with Jesus. He'll lead us to love people well, but He also knows our capacity and His priorities for us.

THE FEAR OF THE LORD IS THE BEGINNING OF WISDOM

Anxiety is often the result of being double-minded. For example, when part of me wants to take one course of action but I'm scared of judgment, it results in an internal conflict. However, when we surrender to Jesus as Lord of our lives, decisions get simpler; we have only Him to please. Inner and spiritual freedom means accepting that people won't always agree with or like our choices. This is where our faith kicks in; Jesus promised that we'd be rewarded for our faith and obedience to Him.

Persecution for our faith often comes in the form of accusations meant to elicit guilt and shame. For example, religious leaders accused Jesus of breaking God's law by healing on the Sabbath. They accused Him of pride and rebellion against the Father by calling Himself the Son of God. But Jesus lived His life before the eyes of the Father, not man.

If we're governed by the fear of man instead of the fear of God, which is the beginning of wisdom (Proverbs 9:10), we'll find it difficult to withstand intimidation. So when we're charged with being foolish, deceived, and haters because we stand by the Word of God, we must know how to bring the charges to the Father and release ourselves from false guilt.

BREAK FREE FROM THE FEAR OF MAN

We can be susceptible to control and manipulation in a church setting because we desire to please God and our spiritual leaders. It's not uncommon for those whose emotional needs are not met by family to crave the approval and acceptance of their church family.

> "Fear and intimidation is a trap that holds you back. But when you place your confidence in the Lord, you will be seated in the high place." (Proverbs 29:25 TPT)

It's easier than we imagine to confuse how God sees us with how our leaders see us. Consciously, we may know the difference, but we can take on messages that "if we love God, we will be people who do…" and end up believing God isn't happy unless we conform to the expectations of our church. It can lead to us devoting more time and resources than is wise to alleviate guilt.

We each have responsibility for wisely using our time, money, gifts, and abilities. While some church environments can be unhealthy, it's ultimately our responsibility to steward our resources well. If we're struggling to put boundaries in place or say no, we may need counselling or inner healing to build our capacity for healthy assertiveness.

When we build a strong relationship with the Lord and can discern His will regarding the choices before us, we're building our house on the rock (Matthew 7:24). The Lord should primarily meet our need for approval and significance. There will be times when doing what's pleasing to the Lord will bring persecution or disapproval from man. Freedom from control requires the ability to withstand people's disapproval, even those we love and admire.

I experienced the dangers of approval addiction first-hand. I was very involved in my previous church. I was a part of the leadership team for many years and loved my church family. However, there was a specific day when I realised my thinking was wayward.

I learned on a Saturday afternoon that a lady with whom I'd spent quite a bit of time had died suddenly. To my surprise, I had no emotional reaction. I knew it was odd and couldn't understand my response. The following day, while getting ready for church, the grief suddenly hit me. I was a mess, crying off all my mascara while pulling myself together to be presentable. Yet, in the midst, I sensed the pull from God to stay home and spend time with Him to process my grief.

The reaction of my heart was, *I can't do that. What will my pastor think?*. The desire for my pastor's approval had me hesitating to obey what I knew was God's voice. I knew that leaders staying home from church was frowned upon. I wrestled for a while but eventually decided to stay home and was blessed during a beautiful encounter with God.

I could blame my pastor for 'making me feel' pressure to attend church, but the reality is that he can't 'make' me do anything. My beliefs govern my feelings and decisions. It was *my* desire for his approval that was controlling me. In reality, if I'd spoken with him about the situation, he likely would have encouraged me to stay home. I needed to work on my heart to ensure my desire to follow God's leading was far greater than my desire for approval from any person. We aren't the helpless victims of other people's issues or wishes. The key is uncovering the lies that leave us open to control and manipulation.

HUMILITY

Humility brings another aspect of freedom from people-pleasing. One of my most significant breakthroughs came in learning to let my outer world reflect my inner world. But, again, a symptom of the fear of man, which in essence is pride, is wanting to appear better or nicer than we are. It stems from performing for our identity. There were many times I didn't want to do what was asked, but I didn't want to look unloving or uncaring. I believed I needed to continually display 'loving' traits to be a real daughter of God. Now I was stuck! I usually ended up doing whatever it was but resented every minute. My heart was at odds with my outward appearance.

One day while in just such a bind, I heard God whisper, "Wendy, you're not Jesus, and I don't expect you to be. I know you're not perfect. Sometimes you're still quite selfish, and I'm ok with that. Stop trying to convince others that you're something you're not." Freedom and joy washed over me as I received His words. I was trying to perform my way into maturity. Somehow, I believed that being a Christian meant that I was supposed to be Jesus in every situation, and I hadn't arrived. I realised God was more interested in me being authentic than perfect.

Humility brings a willingness to have others disapprove of you or not see you as you want. We learn to be governed by what God thinks of us and hold on to our sense of identity even when people don't affirm us.

If you don't feel free to say no, your "yes" isn't really yes. The Bible tells us that unless our works are motivated by love, they're meaningless to God. When inwardly we're saying no, but outwardly saying yes, it's most likely our response is fear-driven rather than love-driven. It's fear of the consequences for saying no that's driving your yes.

It can be challenging to say no to people's requests when healing from abuse and control. God takes us through seasons of strengthening our no. He helps us recognise when it's Him leading us rather than fulfilling people's expectations. It doesn't mean we'll forever do nothing that inconveniences us, but we need seasons of learning to say no so that our yes comes from a place of freedom.

THE FATHER'S VOICE COMES WITH THE FRUIT OF THE SPIRIT

> "But the fruit produced by the Holy Spirit within you is divine love in all its varied expressions joy that overflows, peace that subdues, patience that endures, kindness in action, a life full of virtue, faith that prevails, gentleness of heart, and strength of spirit. Never set the law above these qualities, for they are meant to be limitless." (Galatians 5:22-23 TPT)

The fruit of the Spirit are a guidepost to what the Kingdom of God looks, feels, and sounds like. It's how we discern between the two kingdoms. When our ears are trained to hear the voice of criticism, condemnation, and judgment, we can listen to the enemy's voice and think we're hearing from God.

God is love, and His voice releases love even when it's correcting. So therefore, we should feel secure and connected to Him even while being disciplined.

1 Corinthians 13 tells us what love is, and it may be very different from your experience and understanding of love. When someone tells you they love you and then mistreat you, love takes on a different meaning from what God means when He says He loves you. God's love is patient; He isn't quickly angered. His love is kind, wrapped in mercy and grace. So, if you sense that God is impatient with you because you're not getting it right, it's coming from somewhere other than God.

Love perseveres and never gives up. That means God doesn't give up on you. He will never turn away or reject you because you're not getting it quick enough. His love is kind, which means He looks to serve us and take action to help us. His kindness is also *gentle* and keeps no record of wrongs. So, if you think every time you come before the Father, He's checking a list of your failings, you're very mistaken. His love always protects us; He is a place of shelter and covering for us. He is not looking to shame or dishonour you, but the very opposite.

Joy is a fruit of the Spirit. Even when God corrects me, I have found a sense of joy because I'm empowered to change. There's joy in hearing

His voice and being in communion with Him. *Peace* is another hallmark of His voice. When we commune with God and His Kingdom, His presence will bring peace.

THE FATHER'S VOICE COMES WITH A SOLUTION

In the Kingdom of God, discipline isn't about judgment and punishment. As a child of God, you have a loving Father who wants to teach you the path to blessing and fulfilment. He wants you to be like Him, walking in love and righteousness. So he disciplines us to teach us the way forward, not to judge us as evil and worthy of rejection. When God talks to us about our behaviour, He does a few key things. First, He shows us the impact of our behaviour; we become aware of how we affect the hearts of others, ourselves, and God. Then He offers us the way of the Kingdom, bringing clarity and empowering us to change. It's not just knowing what to do but knowing it's something that we *can* achieve through His grace.

There was a time when I began having a glass of wine of an evening. I was going through a difficult time, and it helped me relax. The Father graciously showed me a picture of my future if I didn't change course. I saw myself five years down the track with a drinking problem while the emotional pain I was medicating remained. I sensed if I were willing to bring my emotional pain to Him, He would walk through it with me, bringing healing. It wasn't the promise of a quick fix – I understood it would take time, but I could see myself healed and free in five years instead of having even more problems and pain.

God didn't scold me or tell me I was terrible for drinking alcohol. He didn't communicate anything about my character or faith; He simply showed me where my actions would lead. When God disciplines us, it doesn't hurt our identity. On the other hand, condemnation tells us that we are the problem. Condemnation leaves us feeling powerless and worthless, weighing us down, and leaving us feeling like we aren't good enough to be in God's presence. The Father's discipline draws us close; condemnation creates a barrier to intimacy with Him.

Freedom is possible when we discern the difference between the Father's leading and the enemy's accusations. If we stand firm in our identity as daughters of God and resist the urge to prove ourselves through performance, we'll enter His rest.

Having won the battle against guilt, we're now positioned to take down the giant of intimidation.

Prayer

Father, thank you that Your voice is loving and gentle. I want to know you more, and I ask for greater discernment to distinguish Your voice from the accuser's. Where my ears hear you as harsh and authoritative, please heal them and give me the capacity to hear and see You as You really are. Father, set me free from worrying about what people think of me and help me live my life before Your eyes only. Thank you that You've silenced the voice of my accuser through Christ. Father, give me a greater revelation of the height, depth, width, and breadth of Your love for me. In Jesus' name, Amen.

CHAPTER SIX

Freedom from Intimidation

If we want to live in our authority, we must learn how to discern and defeat the bully of intimidation.

> "For God did not give us a spirit of timidity but a spirit of power and love and self-control". (2 Timothy 1:7 RSV)

Intimidation makes us timid, robbing us of our power, love, and self-control. It seeks to have us exchange our authority for self-protection. Living in the freedom of our God-given authority requires courage. I speak with many women unhappy about how they're treated in relationships but fearful to confront. Dr Phil says, "We teach people how to treat us". When we're scared to embrace our authority and power within relationships, we place the responsibility for change on the other party and even onto God. Many women are praying for God to do what He's already empowered them to do for themselves.

Your Heavenly Father wants you to live from your Kingdom-given authority. He loves you and provides a way of escape, but it requires you to partner with Him and stand in your power. We might wish our oppressors would lay down their whips, apologise for enslaving us, and usher us into the land of plenty. I know I've felt that way. Did you notice, though, that God didn't *soften* Pharoah's heart to make things easy for the Israelites? On the contrary, the Bible says He *hardened* his heart. So why would He do such a thing?

God intends to bring us *out* of Egypt, not make our lives more comfortable *in* Egypt. Coming out of Egypt means recognising the oppression, breaking free from fear and shame, and not allowing ourselves to be controlled and defined by anyone other than God. In bringing the Israelites out of Egypt, God showed Himself strong and victorious over a powerful enemy. He proved trustworthy and able to fulfil His promises, giving the people a reservoir of experience to drink from in hard times. He wanted them free from fear, sure that He set them free and not Pharoah. Even more than that, their rescue was so miraculous that surrounding nations feared the Israelites because they had a mighty God fighting for them.

The process of emerging from slavery exposed their true beliefs. Certain situations trigger our fears and doubts, tempting us to turn back. In these moments, we need to remember that God doesn't orchestrate difficulty in our lives but will use it to strengthen us if we let Him. Romans 8:28 tells us that all things work for our good; God is faithful and will use anything thrown at us to help us. The things that feel like they're going to take us out can become the places of our most significant growth and victory as we cry out to Him for help. God wants His women strong. We are warriors, destined to crush the head of the serpent, and our training ground is our journey out of Egypt. The strength required to journey out is the same strength needed to take possession of our territory in the Promised Land.

It takes courage to walk away from Egypt. That journey is one of breaking agreement with the deception that seeks to take our power. It's breaking free from the lie that it's wrong to have authority over our own lives and choices. Whether in family relationships, church service, or the workplace, intimidation masquerades as truth but acts like a thief. God will make a safe passage for us from religion, control, and oppression, but we must be willing to stand in truth as we journey out.

CONTROL THROUGH INTIMIDATION

Intimidation uses *fear* to control and is the province of bullies. Most of us have met people who use intimidation to meet their needs. The irony is that it's a form of self-protection rooted in a deep sense of unworthiness. You've probably heard of the fight, flight, freeze response to danger. These protective mechanisms come from a part of the brain that operates subconsciously. We evaluate whether fight (anger) or flight (fear) is our best option in milliseconds. The subconscious evaluation mechanism is primarily determined in early childhood and informed by trauma later in life.

These reactions happen almost instantly, and we feel anger or fear. If we go to anger, we may intimidate those around us, and when others are angry or intimidating, we may shrink back in fear. Conflict makes many people feel unsafe and triggers these defence mechanisms.

PASSIVITY IS A FORM OF DEFENCE

Have you ever found yourself becoming passive when intimidated? Passive behaviour includes avoiding conflict and finding it challenging to be honest about our opinions, emotions, and desires. This often leads to resentment and frustration because we don't feel free to be fully us. Overcoming intimidation is vital for our wellbeing and the health of our relationships.

If you recognise yourself in this, don't panic. You can be free. I've been on the journey of overcoming intimidation, and I've gained crucial insights that I will share with you. First, I want to stress that we must determine whether fear in a relationship stems from a *real* or *perceived* threat. In other words, are you at risk of harm in this relationship? If there is physical, sexual, or emotional violence, your first goal is to be safe. **Your safety is the priority.** Talk with a professional who can help you create a safety plan and work with you to achieve a safe relationship or a safe separation. The strategies I'm going to share are for when there is no actual danger—rather, it's fear stemming from lies and wounds in our past.

BE A PEACEMAKER, NOT A PEACEKEEPER

Passivity can masquerade as godliness. We may believe we're peacemakers when we avoid conflict, but the truth is that if we're avoiding conflict out of fear, we may achieve external peace, but it will create inner turmoil. When we don't feel free to express ourselves within a relationship or arena, we're not true to ourselves, creating a divided heart. Avoiding relational conflict makes us a *peacekeeper* rather than a *peacemaker*. True peace happens when we can assert ourselves in our relationships and work through disputes healthily. Yielding to fear and intimidation is not what God intends. Many passages of Scripture confirm that love, not fear, pleases God.

> "If I were to speak with eloquence in earth's many languages, and in the heavenly tongues of angels, yet I didn't express myself with love, my words would be reduced to the hollow sound of nothing more than a clanging cymbal.
>
> And if I were to have the gift of prophecy with a profound understanding of God's hidden secrets, and if I possessed unending supernatural knowledge, and if I had the greatest gift of faith that could move mountains, but have never learned to love, then I am nothing.
>
> And if I were to be so generous as to give away everything I owned to feed the poor, and to offer my body to be burned as a martyr without the pure motive of love, I would gain nothing of value." (1 Corinthians 13:1-3 TPT)

Our outward behaviour may look selfless when under intimidation, but our motive may be self-preservation, not love.

THOSE THAT KNOW THEIR GOD

I believe *knowing God* is the antidote to living under the yoke of fear and intimidation. But what does it mean to *know* God? The Bible tells us that those who know their God will be bold and courageous. Many of us think of 'knowing' in terms of cognitive understanding in our Western culture. But it's so much more than our narrow definition. Biblically, *to know* means "to have a relationship with". The Bible tells us that Adam *knew* Eve, and she bore a son. It's a relational, experiential word.

You may have heard of 'left brain' and 'right brain'. In a general sense, the left brain is the part that learns through communication, reading, writing, listening and so on. It's the logical, analytical aspect of us. Our right brain, on the other hand, is responsible for emotion. It learns through experience. So, when the Bible says that we are to *know* God, we are to experience Him intimately and know His character by experience. This is very different to learning about Him by reading the Bible and listening to other people talk about their experiences. *We overcome fear and intimidation by knowing God intimately.*

We don't get to know God by reading and hearing about Him any more than I can get to know the Prime Minister by reading a biography about him. We need intimate encounters with God to see Him for who He is. We're exposed to so much Christian teaching, and not all of it reflects God's heart. Intimacy with God helps us discern and resolve false beliefs about His nature and character. Spending time in His presence not only heals our pain, but it builds our faith to trust who He is and how He acts.

As Moses contended with Pharoah to win the Israelite's freedom, things didn't always progress the way he expected. He needed further revelation of the Father's heart before the battle with Pharoah was won. We see it outwork in Exodus 5; God sends Moses to tell Pharoah to let the Children of Israel go. Moses obeys God, and the outcome is even more hardship and a heavier workload for his people. Unsurprisingly, the leaders of Israel complain to Moses.

> "Then, as they came out from Pharaoh, they met Moses and Aaron, who stood there to meet them. And they said to them, "Let the Lord look on you and judge because you have made us abhorrent in the sight of Pharaoh and in the sight of his servants, to put a sword in their hand to kill us." (Exodus 5:20-21 NKJV)

When Moses confronts God about Pharaoh's response and questions why He didn't come through, God's response is interesting. He starts by affirming that He *will* do what He said and tells Moses that He's revealing Himself in a new way.

> "And God spoke to Moses and said to him: "I am the Lord. I appeared to Abraham, to Isaac, and to Jacob, as God Almighty, but by My name Lord I was not known to them." (Exodus 6:2-3 NKJV)

"I am the Lord" is used five times in this chapter. I think God was trying to get something across! *Lord* is the proper name of the one true God. He has no rival; He's the maker of the Heavens and Earth. In this phrase, God brings a revelation of His authority – if *He* says it, nothing can stop it.

Moses struggled because things didn't work out the way he expected. Instead of the answer he *thought* he needed, God gave him a greater revelation of who He was, increasing Moses's faith and authority. Likewise, when we face intimidation and fear that threatens to overwhelm us, we need greater insight into who God is. It's not enough to know intellectually; we need the conviction from spiritual encounters with Him.

LOVE CASTS OUT FEAR

Amid battles, doubts surface, revealing our faith levels and highlighting our need for a greater revelation of His love. Perfect love casts out fear, and our struggle with intimidation exposes our need for an upgrade in *knowing* His love. In these moments, our Father allows us to go from strength to strength and glory to glory.

Generations of slavery and powerlessness in Egypt formed and cemented wrong beliefs about the goodness of God. The Israelites interpreted their pain and mistreatment as evidence that God was okay with their suffering. Time and again, they believed that God was leading them into anguish and torment. They couldn't distinguish between the Egyptians' tyranny and the loving God now leading and providing.

When they arrived at the Red Sea, they complained that God brought them out of Egypt only to kill them. Again, when they couldn't find food, they assumed that God's plan was for them to die in the wilderness. Each time they hit difficulty, their distrust surfaced, revealing their core belief that God was not good. Their captivity blinded them to the true nature of God. He was delivering them out of slavery and into prosperity, honour, and safety, and they resisted Him every step of the way.

God knew they'd find it difficult to trust Him because of the impact of pain and abuse, so why didn't He find a way to resolve it? I believe He did. When God called His people out of Egypt, He said he desired to bring them to Himself. So after they crossed the Red Sea, Moses brought them to Mount Sinai, also known as the Mountain of the Lord. It was here they encountered Him as never before. We need intimacy with God to know Him for who He really is. The way we resolve false beliefs about God is to have face to face encounters with Him. As we spend time in His presence, trauma is healed, our perspective changes, and we can see God for who He is.

God wants to meet with you. He knew that the time in Egypt gave the Israelites a false identity and warped their perception of His nature, so He called them to Himself. He always pursues intimacy with His children. Before they chose rules and religion, the Father walked with Adam and Eve in the garden; this has always been the plan.

People have been choosing rules and religion over intimacy ever since. When the Israelites arrived at Mount Sinai, they feared God. They looked to Moses to stand between them and what they perceived to be an angry God.

> "Then they said to Moses, "You speak with us, and we will hear; but let not God speak with us, lest we die." (Exodus 20:19 NKJV)

Having leaders stand between God and us was never Plan A. When we rely on another person's knowledge or experience of God, it will always be coloured by their perspective. It becomes like Chinese whispers; you gain information, which may or may not be correct.

God's presence and seeing His glory would have healed the powerlessness, fear, and mistrust learned in Egypt. The glory of God is inseparable from His goodness. When we encounter Him in this way, it changes everything. Experiencing the Father's love and witnessing His power and greatness builds faith to face our giants and run toward them confidently, knowing He is with us and will fulfil His promises.

God planned to deliver His people from oppression, transform them through encounters with His presence, and turn them into giant slayers who would possess the Promised Land.

FALSE VIEWS OF GOD

Many of us have unconscious, underlying beliefs about the nature and character of God. As we read the Bible and listen to sermons and teaching, our intellect may tell us God is good, but our hearts can tell a different story. Our relationships with our earthly fathers, authority figures, pastors, and leaders, are some of the ways our hearts learn about our Heavenly Father. It means we'll discover truths about the character of God, but there will likely be false images as well.

Depending on our experiences, particularly in childhood, our hearts will be able to receive God's love and trust Him as our protector or not. I struggled with fear most of my life. I'm sure I would have been diagnosed with social anxiety had I talked with anyone. I remember the day everything changed. It was many years ago now, but it feels like yesterday. I was in prayer, and out of my mouth came, "Father, if there's a blockage in our relationship, could you please reveal it to me?" I was surprised at my words as it hadn't occurred to me that there was any distance between us. The next day I saw so clearly that because there were things in my childhood my father had not protected me from, I didn't believe that my Heavenly Father would protect me either.

I spent time processing this with the Lord, allowing Him to heal the woundedness in my heart. With the blockage resolved, I was amazed at how close I felt to Him. The weight of His presence was tangible, and I knew I wasn't alone. This new intimacy with Father God resolved much of my fear and anxiety. Jesus came to reconcile us to the Father, and until we connect intimately with Him, we may still struggle to feel His protection.

Some common false beliefs about Father God are:

- God isn't really good; He is a punisher.
- God is not powerful enough to protect me.
- God won't defend me because I'm not good enough.
- There's something I need that God will not give me.

> "Love never brings fear, for fear is always related to punishment. But love's perfection drives the fear of punishment far from our hearts. Whoever walks constantly afraid of punishment has not reached love's perfection." (1 John 4:18 TPT)

Our hearts first learn about our Heavenly Father through our relationship with our dads. If your dad was warm and emotionally safe, you'd find it easier to experience God as loving and kind. If your father was angry or a harsh disciplinarian, you'll likely relate from a place of fear.

Many Christians I speak to are afraid of God because they believe He's a punisher. Aware of their imperfections, and like a child fearing she's in trouble, they hide their hearts. Many agonise over every decision, convinced God will abandon them if they make the wrong choice.

> "The Son of Man has come to give life to all who are lost. Think of it this way: If a man owns a hundred sheep and one lamb wanders away and is lost, won't he leave the ninety-nine grazing the hillside and thoroughly search for the one lost lamb? And if he finds his lost lamb, he rejoices over it, more than over the ninety-nine that never went astray. Now you should understand that it is never the desire of your heavenly Father that a single one of these little ones should be lost." (Matthew 18:11-14 TPT)

The beautiful truth is that God comes after us when we wander off. He leaves the ninety-nine to go looking for the lost one. He doesn't worry about how or why we're lost; He comes after us. After Adam and Eve sinned in the garden, He came looking for them. God won't abandon you when you do the wrong thing. You may feel disconnected from God, but He will never leave you because He's a good Father. If you were disciplined harshly as a child, it will take time and healing to see and experience Him as a loving Father.

Even if we had a loving and protective father, we'll likely encounter authority figures who were less-than-ideal. For example, one of my clients attended a Catholic School in the early 1960s. As an eight-year-old, she experienced the harsh discipline of the nuns, leaving her frightened of them *and* the God they represented. As an older lady who loved and pursued the Lord, her image of Him was distorted by the image formed as a child. She assumed God was like the nuns who taught her, judging her every thought and action. No wonder God didn't feel safe!

Early in my relationship with God, I was confused by the Old Testament. I couldn't reconcile Jesus with a God who seemed angry and unapproachable. I'd hear preaching declaring, "God doesn't see you, He sees Jesus", implying it was a good thing God didn't see me because if He did, I'd be toast! I'd picture myself cowering behind Jesus as He stood between an angry God and me. Other scriptures said God was unchanging, adding to my confusion and distress. I found it best to stay in the New Testament; otherwise, I pulled away from my image of Him.

I now understand that the way God is depicted in the Old Testament has to do with Eve's decision to eat from the tree of the knowledge of good and evil. The two trees represented two systems of relating to God. The tree of life was God's way – through love and intimacy. The other relied on the ability of people to navigate right and wrong, trying to reach God through their effort rather than enjoying intimacy with Him. This is the nature of religion, doing our best to adhere to rules and regulations while hoping to avoid judgment. Eve chose this system, and God honoured her choice.

The old covenant was a religious system based on the knowledge of good and evil. The new covenant represents life – God's original intent for relating with His children. The rules have been done away with through Christ, who fulfilled them perfectly on our behalf. Now that we're restored to an intimate relationship with God and have His Spirit inside us, we learn through connection. The Father draws us into righteousness through the leading of His Spirit rather than an external system of rules.

Jesus and the Father are one. Christ came to show us what the Father is really like.

> "Philip spoke up, "Lord, show us the Father, and that will be all that we need!"
>
> Jesus replied, "Philip, I've been with you all this time, and you still don't know who I am? How could you ask me to show you the Father, for anyone who has looked at me has seen the Father. Don't you believe that the Father is living in me and that I am living in the Father? Even my words are not my own but come from my Father, for he lives in me and performs his miracles of power through me. Believe that I live as one with my Father and that my Father lives as one with me—or at least, believe because of the mighty miracles I have done." (John 14:8-11 TPT)

The love and care we see in Jesus comes from the Father. We don't have to hide behind Jesus – the Father has open arms toward us, and He's not measuring our every move, ready to pronounce judgment. He is patient and kind and no longer counts our wrongs against us. If we confess our sins, He is faithful to remove them. When we acknowledge them, the charges are moved from us to Jesus because He carried all our sin when He was on the cross.

"For God will never give you the spirit of fear, but the Holy Spirit who gives you mighty power, love, and self-control." (2 Timothy 1:7 TPT)

YOU ARE POWERFUL

When we suffer abuse, bullying or trauma, particularly in childhood, it can programme us to believe we're powerless and weak. Even if we're not conscious of our powerless thinking, it impacts our approach to life. There's a famous experiment in which scientists placed fleas in a glass jar. The fleas naturally jump much higher than the jar. After being in a closed jar for three days, the fleas were conditioned to jump lower than the lid to avoid hitting it. After their release, the fleas continued to jump only as high as the closed jar.[1]

It's a powerful illustration of how our past can create a powerless mindset. The impact of over 400 years of slavery on God's people left them resistant to entering the Promised Land. The Lord promised them an inheritance; they just needed to trust and do what He said. But fear got the better of them, and they balked. They hit the limit of their trust and tried to find their own way. They chose to walk away rather than face the giants and take possession of God's promised best for them.

The renewing of our minds transforms us. The children of Israel could have entered their inheritance much sooner if they'd allowed a loving God to change their mindsets. Instead, they spent unnecessary time in the wilderness because they couldn't make the transition from slavery to sonship. When the Children of Israel saw the giants in the land, they saw themselves weak and powerless. They shrunk back from the battle because they expected defeat instead of God's promised victory.

> "There we saw the giants (the descendants of Anak came from the giants), and we were like grasshoppers in our own sight, and so we were in their sight." (Numbers 13:33 NKJV)

What an assumption! And yet later, in Joshua, Rahab tells them the nations feared them because they heard what God did to Pharaoh in delivering them from Egypt. Their perception of themselves was the opposite of their enemy. Bill Johnson of Bethel Church, Redding, often says " I can't afford to have thoughts in my head about me that God doesn't have in His.[2] Accepting the truth of who God says you are will take you from a place of fear to one of courage. All creation is waiting for you to get a revelation of who you are! The Earth is waiting for you to take your place as a daughter of God, bringing your realm of influence under God's authority.

> "For the eagerly awaiting creation waits for the revealing of the sons and daughters of God." (Romans 8:19 NASB)

For many years I was intimidated and felt oppressed by various leaders. I'd cry to the Lord, expecting Him to change them, so I didn't have to face opposition and take up my authority. But time and time again, He encouraged me to rise up and stand firm in the face of intimidation. He'd gently remind me He was with me and not to shy away from confrontation when it was required. God has given us everything we need to overcome intimidation; power, love, and self-control.

If we understood how powerful we are, fear would be a thing of the past. The Bible tells us that we've been given a Spirit of power, the Holy Spirit, who He lives inside us. It means we have the power that raised Jesus from the grave residing in us, available 24/7. If we only consider our strength and ability, we'll feel ill-equipped and small. Training ourselves to accept God's miraculous power in us and for us will change our response to intimidation.

> "Yet even in the midst of all these things, we triumph over them all, for God has made us to be more than conquerors, and his demonstrated love is our glorious victory over everything!" (Romans 8:37 TPT)

To be "more than a conqueror" means to win a decisive victory. You have access to the supernatural power of God for every situation you face. You may not *feel* like a conqueror, but you are. Learning to overcome intimidation involves understanding who God is, who you are and how much you are loved. As you connect with God's love, kindness, and power, living from your God-given authority becomes second nature. You can begin to take back the ground that's been stolen and exchange the slavery mindset for your identity as a daughter of God.

Prayer

Father, thank you for being my protector. You are for me, so who could be against me? Please reveal any areas of intimidation I'm living under and expose any lies empowering the fear. Show me the height, depth, width, and breadth of your love. Thank you that your perfect love casts out my fear. I ask for the wisdom and understanding of how to be free in any relationships marked by intimidation. Please show me when to walk away, when to stand, and how to take back my authority. Father, bring the people and resources I need to walk out of oppression and into the freedom of your Kingdom. In Jesus' Name, Amen.

CHAPTER SEVEN

Realms of Authority

Living under authority while staying free from oppression and abuse requires wisdom. The knowledge of good and evil would have us take a principle and apply it to every situation. But the tree of life has us seek God's wisdom and direction for every circumstance, living in constant connection. I'll share some thoughts and experiences in this chapter, but there are no hard and fast rules; it's all about relationship.

A few years ago, while spending time with God, I sensed His deep longing for connection with His children. However, I could see a barrier that made that connection difficult; it wasn't a solid barrier but was a hindrance. When I asked Him what it was, He replied, "leadership". I was initially stunned, but I understand how easy it is to have an unhealthy relationship with leadership, especially when we elevate them to a level they were never intended to occupy.

Jesus taught us not to call each other 'teacher' or 'father' because we're all brothers and sisters (John 23:8-12). The apostle John affirmed we don't need others to teach us because we have the Holy Spirit.

> "But the wonderful anointing you have received from God is so much greater than their deception and now lives in you. There's no need for anyone to keep teaching you. His anointing teaches you all that you need to know, for it will lead you into truth, not a counterfeit. So just as the anointing has taught you, remain in him." (1 John 2:27 TPT)

Again, Scripture brings balance, so we don't take the truth to an unhealthy extreme. God has given us leaders and shepherds to *help* and *serve*, using their gifts to help guide us in our spiritual journey.

> "Obey your spiritual leaders and recognise their authority, for they keep watch over your soul without resting since they will have to give an account to God for their work. So it will benefit you when you make their work a pleasure and not a heavy burden." (Hebrews 13:17 TPT)

When we see leaders abuse power, it's tempting to reject all authority. Unfortunately, the misuse of power is so prevalent that many people never experience Godly leadership. For those who've lived under controlling, selfish leaders, the very word 'submit' makes them shudder.

Corrupt governments, controlling church leaders, and abusive husbands have given rise to a culture that disdains authority. While it may seem the only option, it leaves us in a very vulnerable position. Leaders and authorities are God's idea for the wellbeing of those under them, not the detriment.

Jesus and the apostles taught us to submit to the governing authorities (Romans 13:1-7, Titus 3:1). When Jesus was asked whether people should pay taxes or not, He indicated there's a place for government and that people should respect governmental authority (Mark 12:13-17). Jesus made the point that being part of the Kingdom of God did not give licence to disregard the laws of the land.

A LESSON IN KINGDOM AUTHORITY

Ray was friends with my eldest brother Michael. He'd become a Christian around the same time as me and owned a business next door to our motel. Ray started attending our Church and came along to the weekly Bible studies. He was dealing with the breakup of his marriage and the resulting separation from his three young children.

One day, after Bible study, Ray asked me out. I was caught entirely off guard and didn't know how to respond. I wasn't interested in a romantic relationship; I loved Jesus and wanted to focus my time and attention on Him. "I'll have to pray about it" was my vague and non-committal response. Poor Ray, I was zealous as a new Christian and determined to live my life differently. After years of doing things my way and reaping pain, I was excited to have a loving Father who could help me make wise decisions, and I didn't want to make a move without prayer.

After praying for a few days, I felt comfortable going out on a date with Ray. Our hearts connected, and I cared deeply for him. We started seeing each other, often going for coffee after Bible study or catching up for meal breaks at work.

After a few weeks, I felt myself pulling away. Foreboding replaced my initial peace about the relationship. I didn't understand why I felt this way and assumed God was telling me the relationship wasn't a good idea. Finally, I decided to break it off and planned to do it after Bible study. I was gathering the courage to tell him as we had our traditional coffee when I felt the presence of God beside me. I turned, expecting to see an angel or Jesus as the presence was so tangible.

A flow of love emanating from God's heart filled mine till I thought it would burst. I then sensed it flowing out of my heart toward Ray. I was speechless. I'm not sure what my face was doing, but Ray asked me what was happening. I tried to explain but couldn't find the words. I was reeling but knew I'd been mistaken and that God wasn't leading me to end the relationship.

The next day I asked the Lord to tell me why I hadn't had peace about the relationship. Once again, I felt the strong presence of the Lord beside me. First, I saw myself as a young girl dreaming of my knight in shining armour. Then I saw myself, time after time, being rejected, used, and hurt in relationships. As I continued to look, Jesus stood beside me, allowing me to see it through His eyes. I saw the little girl yearning for love and acceptance and trying to find in each relationship. There was no judgment, just compassion as He revealed that I'd built a thick wall around my heart and given up on finding love because of the accumulated hurt.

I felt no disapproval from Him. Instead, I sensed His love and compassion for me and realised sin is only sin because it hurts us. God truly is love and any behaviour or attitude of the heart that wars against our soul, He has judged as sin to spare us pain.

Seeing myself in situations before I knew God, I expected to feel the sting of disapproval. But instead, He revealed how my behaviour was hurting me. He knew the need I was trying to fill and showed me the pain my actions inflicted on my heart. It taught me so much about the kind of Father He is. He wants to teach us His ways because they're better for us. The Father wants us to understand the *why* behind His commands, so we will freely choose them.

As I stood there with Jesus, I understood I wanted to pull away from Ray because the next step was to take my wall down and give him access to my heart. I was scared to make myself vulnerable, and fear told me to run away. I'm amazed at how much happens on a subconscious level. I'm very grateful that God sees all and knows when to reveal these things to us. As I stood with Him, I decided to bring the wall down. I felt safe with Jesus. He comforted me as I let the pain surface and then flow. I felt very different afterwards—my heart felt free. Ray and I kept dating and enjoying getting to know each other.

GOD WORKS IN MYSTERIOUS WAYS

Around six months into dating, the Lord asked me to lay the relationship down. I didn't understand why, and I didn't want to do it. Finally, I decided to obey but did so with an attitude of "You're making me do this, you're mean, and I'm not happy!" I spoke to Ray and broke it off. He was very hurt, and I couldn't cope with seeing his pain, so I caved and reconciled within days.

I had no peace about my decision, and within a month, God again asked me to end the relationship. This time I approached it differently. I asked the Lord if I'd missed Him from the start and if the relationship was never His best for me. I sensed Him say I'd followed His lead, and now He was asking me to do this. When I asked why He said that there would be treasures greater than gold awaiting if I dared to trust and obey. I felt His love for Ray and a profound certainty that He wouldn't ask me to do anything against Ray's best interests, even if it meant short term pain. Approaching it humbly and seeing through the lens of God's love empowered me to obey.

I knew that it wouldn't be easy for either of us. So I prayed for the strength to do what I knew God was asking of me. When I told Ray, and in the weeks following, it was as if there was a shield over my heart protecting me from the emotional impact. I felt a supernatural strength and knew the Lord answering my prayer for help.

I learned so much about accessing God's power and grace (supernatural empowerment to obey) during this time. The first time I tried to lay the relationship down with Ray, I couldn't access His grace because of my attitude. I obeyed without an understanding of God's heart towards Ray or me. I was following a rule rather than understanding His love. However, as I chose to trust my loving Father (even though I still didn't understand), I had supernatural power to do what He asked.

> "Our faith guarantees us permanent access into this marvellous kindness that has given us a perfect relationship with God. What incredible joy bursts forth within us as we keep on celebrating our hope of experiencing God's glory!" (Romans 5:2 TPT)

Faith grants us access to the power of God. Therefore, confidence in the nature and character of God is crucial, and we must view everything through the lens of His love.

A few weeks later, I was working the evening shift. Ray had gone out to dinner with my sister Joanne. They'd become friends, and Jo was checking up to make sure he was okay. As I worked that night, I felt the guard around my heart leave. I sensed God say it was okay to renew our relationship. On the one hand, I was excited but, on the other, disappointed as I still didn't understand the reason for the separation in the first place. I prayed Ray would know God was leading me, and it wasn't just me thinking crazy thoughts!

After dinner, Ray dropped by. He told me that during his conversation with Jo, he felt God challenged him to change some things in our relationship, and as a result, his thinking was shifting. I knew this was the breakthrough God wanted to bring. It was the confirmation I'd prayed for at the very moment Ray's thinking was being transformed. I knew God was telling me it was right for us to reunite.

I'm so grateful to God for taking me through the process. It was vital for me to know I'd put God above all else, even when I didn't understand or want what He asked of me. Surrendering to God in every area of life is the pathway to His best for our lives.

Twelve months in, we decided to marry. We went to our pastor to ask if he would do the honours. He asked us to meet weekly with him and his wife to discuss things. I assumed it was pre-marriage counselling, but before our first meeting, I sensed the Lord say people were judging from the outside, but only He knows the heart. I didn't understand what he meant, but it soon became apparent. My pastor and his wife didn't believe our relationship was of God, and the purpose of the meeting was to convince us not to marry.

I was bewildered by their response, but I'd been a Christian for a little over twelve months, while my pastor had known God for more years than I'd been alive. I looked up to him and believed that his motives were pure. I explained my encounters and how I'd sought God's guidance at every step, but they didn't believe I'd heard from God. Worse than that, they told me I was too young in the faith to be able to distinguish between God and the devil, so I was deceived. They said we should have brought the relationship to them at the start because God speaks through church leaders.

The ramifications were enormous. If I couldn't hear from God as I sought Him with all my heart, what did that mean for my relationship with Him? All that was left was to sit on a pew each week and go through the motions of religion. I wrestled week after week, questioning everything I believed about God. If what my pastor said was true, I had nothing, and my whole Christian life was a farce. I couldn't believe it was right, and yet how could a man of God get it so wrong? Was I prideful in thinking I knew better than him?

I prayed, fasted, and sought God for answers. And yet, the question remained; *if I'm hearing from the devil, what's the point in praying?* I knew I was willing to do whatever God asked of me. I broke off my relationship with Ray when He had asked me to, so why would He not make Himself heard when His daughter asked for guidance?

One day as I sat on my couch praying, I felt His answer come. His voice was powerful, strong, and unmistakable. "Wendy, don't EVER follow a man. Follow ME! My sheep know My voice." I realised that although God gives the Body of Christ leaders, pastors, and teachers for our equipping, they must never take the place of our relationship with Him. Further, I realised He had met with me powerfully during our courtship so that I had the strength to stand firm. Our Heavenly Father always equips us for any testing or trial we face.

We continued to meet with our pastor and his wife for a few weeks, hoping to work it through. Again, I was honest about how I saw things. It came to a point where they said the only way forward was to repent for the relationship and start afresh. I thought and prayed about this and knew I couldn't agree because I didn't believe it was wrong. I could pretend to repent and go through the motions, but that was dishonest. It became clear there was no way forward, and so Ray and I left the Church and found a pastor who, after hearing our story, was happy to marry us.

Our wedding was a wonderful celebration, and I loved being married to the man of my dreams. But in stark contrast, my relationship with the Lord started to deteriorate. The situation with our pastors had been so distressing and confusing that once I'd heard from the Lord on the matter, I shut my heart to His voice, even though I knew there were still unresolved issues.

Little did I know—you can't shut God out of one part of your heart and not have it compromise the rest of your relationship. As I put walls up, my heart grew cold. Ray and I looked for another church. We visited many, but none felt like home. For close to two years, we didn't fellowship anywhere regularly. I didn't realise how much I'd backslidden because it was gradual, and I wasn't connecting with anyone who was really on fire for God.

God is kind and faithful when we're faithless. One night I had a dream that shook me into reality. There was a giant spiral slide with different levels to exit and walk down the stairs. The closer to the ground it got, the steeper it became. God said, "If you don't get off now, it will be so steep it will be beyond your ability to get off." When I woke, I knew He was warning that if I didn't open my heart and turn back to Him, I might not be able to down the track.

Although God never turns away from us, when we put walls up and resist the Holy Spirit, our hearts harden, and we eventually lose the capability to hear Him. I knew things were unresolved from our previous Church, and I needed to understand more. So, I stood before the Father and opened my heart to listen to His voice.

THE GODLY ORDER OF KINGDOM AUTHORITY

Over the next few days, the Lord began to teach me about authority in the Kingdom of God using a business model. In a business, there's a chain of command. Most organisations have an organisational chart—a diagram displaying the lines of authority and responsibility.

There's a clear line of authority with the owner having ultimate responsibility for the company's success. They'll ultimately be held to account if the law is broken or the business owes money.

The owner delegates some authority to the general manager responsible for the day-to-day running. The general manager has the authority to give direction and correction to the chef because he's accountable for the results. Their authority is the power and right to enforce directives with consequences if the chef fails to do what's asked. For example, he may withhold bonuses or even fire them if they don't submit to the delegated authority of the manager.

This delegated authority model means not everyone in the organisation has to know or do everything. As a result, it allows diversity and greater productivity as people focus on specific roles and accountabilities.

Jesus showed me that **He** is the head of the Church and He's appointed pastors and leaders who carry His delegated authority. I chose to trust Him, knowing He would intervene to bring about His will for me if I committed myself to Him. In His infinite wisdom, God makes a way for the Body of Christ to be in unity, allowing for different maturity levels and a diversity of gifts and callings. Godly order and leadership enable people to move together as the family of God.

PROTECTION

I started to understand that authority is also for my protection. It provides checks and balances to ensure I'm hearing from God and not led astray by leaning on my own understanding (Proverbs 3:5).

Just as children have parents to guide them until they can make wise decisions, Godly leaders who see the bigger picture can help keep us safe from harm. We need to trust Jesus to work through His delegated lines of authority within His Church. In my situation, even though my pastors were incorrect, I should have submitted to them and prayed for God to guide them. I felt the Lord say that had I surrendered to their request, He would have shown them His will. The outcome would have been far better, with less negative impact, particularly on my relationship with the Lord.

I shut things down too quickly. God wanted me to endure and wait for Him to come through for me. Instead, I took matters into my own hands and withdrew from the process. God wanted me to submit to authority, even though they weren't accurately discerning His will. There are processes we go through to develop godly character. They're often confusing and painful, but if we learn to love and trust God, He'll transform us into mature followers of Christ.

Had God used a situation where I was wrong, and the pastors were right, I wouldn't have learned to submit to authority. I'd still believe I should only submit if they agree with me. Instead, God taught me to submit as an act of faith in Jesus as my head. My confidence wasn't in the leaders but Him. When I look to Him as head of His Church, my faith invites Him to intervene, bringing order to my disorder.

Hear me rightly; following leaders blindly is not what God asks of us. Christianity is a relational journey, and we must bring every situation to God as we listen for His voice and follow His direction. I knew I needed to put things right with my previous pastors, so I reached out and asked to meet with them. I asked for forgiveness for not journeying with them through the process and shared what I'd learned about submission to Kingdom authority. We could now settle into a church home with the issue behind us. It was as if God said, "I'm not going to allow you to be a part of my body until you've dealt with this issue and understand how to relate to my delegated authority."

RELATING TO CHURCH AUTHORITY

I now relate to leadership through the lens of faith. It's my responsibility to hear from God for my life and pursue my calling. When I sense God is leading me in a new direction or talking to me about big decisions, I ask Him to confirm through relevant authority figures in my life. I put the ball in God's court. "If this is You Lord, you need to speak to Ray because I'm not going to fight him to get my way." If I don't get a green light, I conclude that I've misheard, or perhaps the timing isn't right.

If it's connected to a church ministry, I ask God to speak to my pastor. If God has asked me to do something in a Church context, it's His responsibility to make a way within the leadership. My part is to pray into the vision before bringing it before my leaders. Engaging with the process and working things through with leaders teaches us humility and love, the keys to promotion.

If we don't have some form of accountability in our lives, we're in a dangerous place. We all have blind spots and need trusted people we invite to speak the truth to us. If I only trust myself and my ability to hear God, there's no way God can correct me. I've seen Christians fall into deception because they wouldn't allow anyone to speak into their lives. Instead, they listened to the voice they believed to be God and trusted it over and above every other, leaving them exposed and susceptible.

It's easy to err on one side or the other. I found myself putting all my trust in my pastor and blindly submitting or disregarding him entirely and doing it my way. When we value unity, we'll be willing to walk through the often-lengthy process required to resolve differences. As John Bevere says, "Submission doesn't begin **until** there is disagreement."[1] If we only submit when we agree, we're not in a place of protection. However, if we blindly follow leaders, our relationship with the Church and people ends up taking precedence over our relationship with our loving Father.

AUTHORITY 101

I found that getting clarity on a few key areas helped clear up grey areas when relating to authority. We must first see how responsibility and authority are linked. If I hold responsibility for something, I need authority to make decisions in that area. For example, there are particular responsibilities a manager has for which they're accountable. Many businesses tie Key Performance Indicators (KPIs) to roles so they can measure the performance of employees against specific outcomes.

If a manager consistently underperforms against KPIs, they may be disciplined and eventually lose their job. Managers have authority so they can produce the desired results for the company. If they're not given power, their ability to meet KPIs is compromised, leaving them responsible for outcomes beyond their ability to deliver.

Imagine you're a restaurant manager, with your ongoing employment tied to the restaurant's profitability. Unfortunately, your chef is an alcoholic who regularly doesn't show up for work. When he does, the quality of his food is terrible, and the restaurant is losing customers and money. But your employer won't let you discipline him in any way.

You're hamstrung because you don't have the power or authority to deliver the desired and required outcome. I've counselled many people facing this kind of scenario, and it causes a great deal of distress and frustration.

We need authority in the areas for which we're accountable. For example, when considering whether we should submit to another person or make our own decision, it's helpful to think about who is responsible for the outcome. Who will give an account for the consequences? This defines the realm of authority.

REALMS OF AUTHORITY SNAPSHOT

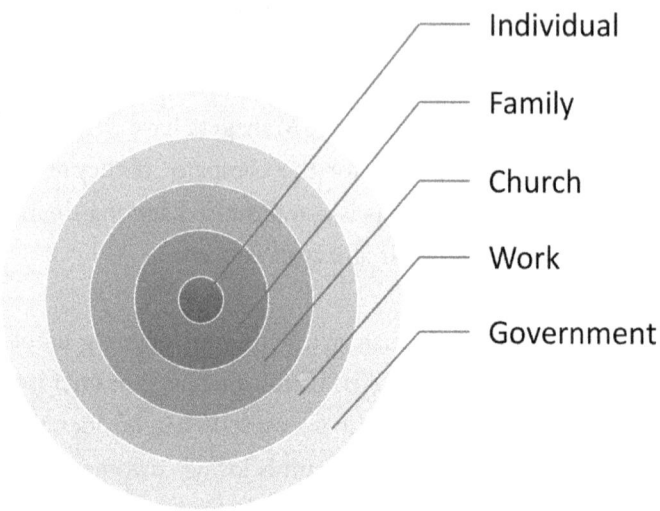

Government

Government leaders and officials have a realm of authority over communities and nations. In Australia, we have three levels of government – local, state, and federal, each with its authority and responsibility.

We're instructed in Scripture to obey the laws of the land. However, if the government's laws require us to disobey the Word of God, we're expected to obey God rather than the government.

Business

There's a realm of authority extending over the workplace. Laws govern what can be asked of you. In addition, there are contracts, workplace agreements, and industry awards that govern the scope of your rights and responsibilities.

Church

Pastors and leaders have a realm of authority within the Church. When the Lord gives someone an assignment, they are accountable for the outcome. For this reason, the one given the assignment is the one with the authority to make the decisions.

For example, suppose a church member wants to start a ministry. In that case, the pastor has legitimate authority to decide whether it should happen within their community because they're the ones entrusted with the vision from God.

Family

Husbands and wives have a realm of authority within the family. God's Word teaches that the husband is the family leader, yet we are encouraged to submit to each other in love.

> "for the husband provides leadership for the wife, just as Christ provides leadership for his Church, as the Saviour and Reviver of the body. In the same way the Church is devoted to Christ, let the wives be devoted to their husbands in everything.
>
> And to the husbands, you are to demonstrate love for your wives with the same tender devotion that Christ demonstrated to us, his bride. For he died for us, sacrificing himself" (Ephesians 5:23-25 TPT)

The husband's role is to empower and protect his wife and children. Just as Jesus laid down His life for His bride, husbands are called and anointed to love their families, putting their needs first. The husband's realm of authority does not impinge on the individual authority of the wife, and God intends that there is mutual honour and submission.

> "And out of your reverence for Christ, be supportive of each other in love.
>
> Both the husband and the wife have a realm of authority over their children.
>
> Children, if you want to be wise, listen to your parents and do what they tell you, and the Lord will help you.
>
> For the commandment, "Honor your father and your mother," was the first of the Ten Commandments with a promise attached: "You will prosper and live a long, full life if you honor your parents." (Ephesians 6:1-2 TPT)

Parental authority is time-limited. There is an age at which children come out from under their parent's management and are legally responsible for themselves.

Individual Responsibility

Each of us has a realm of authority and responsibility before God. We're accountable for our own decisions. Others may ask or even demand that we go against our conscience, but we're free to choose and bear the ultimate responsibility. It may mean there will be times when we decide not to follow the directives of those in authority over us.

I was faced with this scenario soon after starting a new job. My manager told me to lie to the customers regarding a discount card that the company no longer wanted to honour. He was my boss, and he gave a clear directive, but it went against my core values and the Word of God. If I lied, I was responsible for my choice and accountable for my actions. I respectfully told my manager that I was a Christian and wasn't going to lie. I told him I'd be willing to pass those customers to another staff member, but I'd need to leave the company if that wasn't an option. I spoke with respect and humility, not threatening but communicating my values and the options. Management permitted me to pass the calls on to another staff member, and it wasn't long before they scrapped the policy. I continued to work in the business for many years, enjoying a great relationship with the senior management.

In Egypt, Pharoah directed the midwives to kill all the male children of the Israelites. They refused to obey him because they feared God more than Pharoah. Their refusal to obey his authority brought them a blessing.

> "Therefore God dealt well with the midwives, and the people multiplied and grew very mighty. And so it was, because the midwives feared God, that He provided households for them." (Exodus 1:20-21 NKJV)

God is eager to break the chains of oppression and love you into freedom. Yes, it can be scary to leave the security of the familiar, but He is with you. As we walk through the final chapters, we'll address some of the issues that hinder or stop us from entering the Promised Land. If you've lived in Egypt for a long time, the journey will take time. Be patient with yourself as you engage with the process. Remember, the Israelites walked through developing trust in both Moses and God and were led, step by step, into freedom and rest.

Prayer

Father, thank you for the leaders You've placed in my life for my protection and empowerment. I ask for wisdom to recognise where each realm of authority starts and ends. Teach me your ways and show me how to relate to power. Thank you for Your grace and protection as I grow and learn. Father, please dissolve any strongholds or mindsets formed from false teaching. Give me new eyes to see how Kingdom authority operates. Help me take up my authority while submitting to the governing authorities as You desire. Increase my understanding and wisdom so I can align with Your Kingdom in every area of my life. In Jesus' Name, Amen.

CHAPTER EIGHT

Kingdom Marriages

God designed Eve to be both a 'helper' and companion to Adam. Like so many before me, I once believed that 'helper' was less than—a secondary position. I thought that as my husband's helper, my calling was to help him fulfil his destiny. In my mind, it made his calling *the* calling and reduced me to an extension of him. While we need to love and serve our husbands and families with humility, I was left with the distinct impression that I was less critical in the scheme of things.

I was surprised and relieved to learn that God is also described as a *helper to humanity* (Psalm 54:4, Isaiah 41:10, Hebrews 13:6). And in John 14:26, Jesus portrayed Holy Spirit as our helper. Can you imagine trying to do life without the help of the Holy Spirit? Jesus was filled with and led by Holy Spirit, and the same is available to us.

Jesus taught that humanity would be better off when He returned to the Father because He would send the Holy Spirit to us. How beautiful is the way Jesus honours Holy Spirit over Himself? Then we see Holy Spirit revealing Jesus to us. Jesus came to show the Father, and the Father honours Jesus. In the Godhead, we have a beautiful picture of partnership in how Jesus, the Father, and the Holy Spirit love one another without competition or hierarchy.

There's something for us to learn about the heart and nature of God in the way they work together in different roles with humility and honour, each yielding and directing our attention to the other.

> "But the Helper (Comforter, Advocate, Intercessor—Counsellor, Strengthener, Standby), the Holy Spirit, whom the Father will send in My name [in My place, to represent Me and act on My behalf], He will teach you all things. And He will help you remember everything that I have told you". (John 14: 26 AMP)

We're not designed to do life alone, and God intended for men and women to help strengthen one another in the closest of relationships. So, the roles each fulfil are different but complementary.

Although I saw my role as inferior for many years, it brought me joy to serve my family, learning to love them well. I did it in faith and held on to scriptures telling me not to tire of doing good because, in due season, I'd reap what I'd sown (Galatians 6:9). Over time, God showed me areas where my understanding of His heart for women and marriage was misguided. He challenged me to change some aspects of my behaviour. As I changed, it led to Changes in Ray's attitude and behaviour.

The result is a beautiful mutuality in our relationship where we each desire to see the other fulfil their God-given destiny and purpose. We both lend our strengths and gifts to see the other succeed and prosper. The years of sowing have been followed by years of reaping, and my husband's love is evidenced in his willingness to pour his time and finances into helping me fulfil my dreams.

FALLEN MINDSETS

Sadly, the beautiful picture of mutuality and honour of God's design is lacking in many Christian marriages. I speak with many men and women whose image of a Godly marriage is taken from the Fall rather than God's original plan.

> "To the woman He said,
> "I will greatly multiply
> Your pain in childbirth,
> In pain you shall deliver children;
> Yet your desire will be for your husband,
> And he shall rule over you." (Genesis 3:16 NASB)

One of the consequences of the Fall of humanity was that a woman's longing would be for her husband and that he would rule over her. It's important to understand that this wasn't in God's original plan. To rule over someone means to gain control over them or gain dominion. It's so far from the mutual honour and respect we've just talked about. When we're living under this mindset, it's like we have a veil over our eyes and see everything through a hierarchical paradigm.

Jesus set us free from the curse when He died on the cross and rose again from the grave. Every consequence was put on Him, and He made a way to restore God's original Kingdom design. As Christians, we no longer have to live with the repercussions of our rebellion.

The belief that it's God's plan for husbands to rule their wives can lead to the tolerating of abusive relationships. The idea that God is pleased when women submit to control and abuse disable women's instinct for safety and security for themselves and their children. I've counselled many Christian women suffering in abusive marriages. It's always distressing to see daughters of the Most High God enduring circumstances a world away from His design for marriage.

What saddens me the most is that many believe they're pleasing God by accepting the disrespect, neglect, and abuse. Not only are they tricked into suffering needlessly, but it also skews their understanding of His nature. I've lost count of the number of women who come for counselling, seeking to change *their* behaviour to appease their husbands. Others come believing if they could be more Christlike, the relationship would somehow heal. Others hope to 'fix' themselves so they can be 'worthy" of love and emotional connection.

In working with these clients, I find most take on the full responsibility for issues in their marriage and feel guilty for not fixing it. But, on the flip side, nearly all of them resist any confrontation with their spouse and reject separation as an acceptable option.

In this chapter, we'll explore some of the reasons women find it difficult to recognise they're under oppression. Many are trying to fix the problem of being in Egypt by working harder to avoid the beatings instead of leaving Egypt. Escaping Egypt doesn't necessarily mean leaving the marriage; it often means taking back power and refusing accountability for things that aren't their responsibility. The first step is to identify the lies keeping us in bondage.

Humans tend toward extremes, while God's way is usually somewhere in the middle. I believe all truth is held in tension. When certain scriptures are overemphasised, it creates an off-balance culture and doesn't reflect the Father's heart. There are seeming contradictions in the Bible, but these opposing verses enable God to balance our theology, avoiding harmful extremes. My own journey around Kingdom authority has been one of constant adjustment. I've tended to learn a principle and then apply it to every situation, creating rigid rules. That's not God's heart. Our Father doesn't want us enslaved to rules but to understand and walk in His loving ways.

Misunderstandings and extreme views around submission, forgiveness, the sanctity of the marriage covenant, and doctrines about laying down our rights often leave women feeling powerless.

SUBMISSION

Scripture is often taught with an underlying assumption that women are emotionally and psychologically strong and simply need to learn to let go of control. The truth is that one in three women have experienced childhood or relationship abuse, leaving them feeling powerless. When submission is taught this way, it pushes women further into unhealthy levels of compliance.

The problem is that submission *is* a biblical concept. However, when read in context and through the lens of Paul's declaration that all are equal in the eyes of God (Galatians 3:28), a different picture emerges.

> "For wives, this means being devoted to your husbands like you are tenderly devoted to our Lord, for the husband provides leadership for the wife, just as Christ provides leadership for his church, as the Saviour and Reviver of the body. In the same way the church is devoted to Christ, let the wives be devoted to their husbands in everything.
>
> And to the husbands, you are to demonstrate love for your wives with the same tender devotion that Christ demonstrated to us, his bride. For he died for us, sacrificing himself to make us holy and pure, cleansing us through the showering of the pure water of the Word of God. All that he does in us is designed to make us a mature church for his pleasure, until we become a source of praise to him—glorious and radiant, beautiful, and holy, without fault or flaw.
>
> Husbands have the obligation of loving and caring for their wives the same way they love and care for their own bodies, for to love your wife is to love your own self. No one abuses his own body, but pampers it—serving and satisfying its needs. That's exactly what Christ does for his church! He serves and satisfies us as members of his body.

For this reason a man is to leave his father and his mother and lovingly hold to his wife, since the two have become joined as one flesh. Marriage is the beautiful design of the Almighty, a great mystery of Christ and his church. So every married man should be gracious to his wife just as he is gracious to himself. And every wife should be tenderly devoted to her husband." (Ephesians 5:22-33 TPT)

The Apostle Paul has more to say about husbands loving their wives than wives submitting to their husbands. The responsibility for leading the family includes husbands loving and laying down their lives for their wives. As already mentioned, the core purposes of leadership are to empower and protect those under authority. If the role of a husband is as the leader, then his authority is to be used to promote the wellbeing of his wife.

The emphasis on submission over the husband's duty to love sacrificially creates a culture that tolerates oppression, abuse, and domestic violence.

DOMESTIC ABUSE

Intimate partner abuse defies socio-economic, cultural, and religious borders. Domestic violence refers to an abuse of power within close relationships where one person lives in a state of fear and intimidation because of the control exerted by their partner. It often includes a physical power imbalance amplifying the impact in male to female relationships.

Interestingly, many women don't believe "domestic violence" applies to their situation. This is because we narrow the definition to include only the extreme of physical violence when it also includes things like psychological abuse, financial abuse, emotional abuse, and sexual violence.

> *"International surveys have suggested that around one-third of all adult women will, at some point in their lifetime, experience abuse perpetrated by an intimate male partner. Domestic violence is considered to be one of the major risk factors affecting women's health in Australia, and there is a need for the community to respond in ways that reduce the likelihood of further violence occurring."* [1]

Sadly, Christian communities aren't immune, with domestic violence prevalent across all denominations. The overemphasis on a twisted doctrine of submission increases gender inequality and creates a power imbalance between husbands and wives. On top of that, many link suffering in abusive marriages with scriptures encouraging Christians to endure mistreatment for the sake of Jesus.

DOESN'T GOD WANT ME TO SUFFER?

> "Servants, be subject to your masters with all respect, not only to the good and gentle but also to the unjust. For this is a gracious thing, when, mindful of God, one endures sorrows while suffering unjustly. For what credit is it if, when you sin and are beaten for it, you endure?

But if when you do good and suffer for it you endure, this is a gracious thing in the sight of God.

For to this you have been called because Christ also suffered for you, leaving you an example, so that you might follow in his steps. He committed no sin, neither was deceit found in his mouth. When he was reviled, he did not revile in return; when he suffered, he did not threaten, but continued entrusting himself to him who judges justly." (1 Peter 2:18-23 TPT)

What do you see as you read this passage? Do you believe God wants you to suffer unjustly to become more Christlike? I've worked with women who stayed in abusive relationships, believing God sanctioned it. They believed the lie that enduring mistreatment would eventually glorify Him. But how can we reconcile this with a loving Father who sent His Son to give us abundant life? What are the writers really saying through this Scripture and others like it?

The message of the new covenant of Jesus Christ is in stark contrast with the old covenant, where an eye for an eye was the norm. In His Kingdom, injustice and mistreatment are met with God's love, mercy, grace, and justice. The old ways taught retaliation and retribution. In the new covenant, God has placed His Spirit in us, training us as sons and daughters in His ways.

It doesn't mean God wants us to suffer or that we're wrong to create boundaries to protect ourselves from mistreatment. However, *we don't glorify God by tolerating abuse; we glorify God by not sinning if we suffer abuse.*

What NOT to do when you are being mistreated, abused, or controlled,

- Come into agreement with what is said about you or your behaviour
- Retaliate
- Come under intimidation
- Take on false responsibility for the mistreatment
- Think that God wants the abuse or mistreatment to continue

SUBMISSION DOESN'T EQUAL AGREEMENT

You are God's masterpiece! He purposefully and intricately designed you, and He says you're amazing!

> "You formed my innermost being, shaping my delicate inside
> and my intricate outside,
> and wove them all together in my mother's womb.
> I thank you, God, for making me so mysteriously complex!
> **Everything you do is marvelously breathtaking.**
> It simply amazes me to think about it!
> How thoroughly you know me, Lord!
> You even formed every bone in my body
> when you created me in the secret place;
> **carefully, skillfully you shaped me** from nothing to something.
> You saw who you created me to be before I became me!
> Before I'd ever seen the light of day,
> the number of days you planned for me

> were already recorded in your book.
> Every single moment you are thinking of me!
> How precious and wonderful to consider
> **that you cherish me constantly in your every thought!**
> O God, your desires toward me are more
> than the grains of sand on every shore!
> When I awake each morning, you're still
> with me." (Psalm 139:14 TPT)

What God says about us is our true north. If the words of others don't align with His thoughts towards us, we can know they're not from Him. Words are powerful, and verbal abuse can leave scars. If we allow it, they have the power to change our beliefs about ourselves. When authority figures speak hurtful words, they're even more impacting. In addition, the relationships with our parents, spouse, teachers, and Christian leaders, adds weight to their words, making us more inclined to receive what they say.

Regardless of who's speaking, if their words cause us to feel small, ashamed, blamed, and inferior, it's not from God, and we must not take it on. Measure the words of others along with your self-talk against Scripture. Your identity isn't tied to your behaviour. People can change their view of us depending on whether or not they like our behaviour, but God never changes. No matter what, He is a loving Father and your advocate.

Our less than perfect behaviour is forgiven through the cross, and we're free to live in our identity as perfected children of God. Learn to bring everything to the Father in prayer and ask Him to reveal the truth to you. At times you may receive an immediate sense of what the Father is saying; at others, He will answer you over time.

Jesus submitted to authority but never accepted false words about His identity. He knew who He was and never allowed the rejection and ridicule of others to erode His sense of self. The words of His Heavenly Father shaped His identity, so the treatment and assertions of religious leaders didn't change how He saw Himself. When we know who we are and whose we are, we can submit to and respect authority without taking on their opinions.

Choose to come out from under the harsh words, criticisms, and labels others have put on you. Take hold of your God-given identity and never let it go! It will be an anchor in the storm and keep you steadfast in truth. When we choose to hold on to God's truth and our identity in Him, He will use everything people and the enemy throw at us to strengthen us.

OUR TRUE NORTH

Holding on to true north internally when external forces are trying to change your truth requires a strong connection with Holy Spirit and some healthy relationships to help you stay in truth. You get to choose whose words carry weight in your life and whose words you accept, even if you don't feel you can prevent the negativity around you just yet.

Suppose you're in a situation where your identity is daily eroded, and your wellbeing is suffering. In that case, you need to consider removing yourself for at least a time. If your living environment was making you physically ill, I'm sure you wouldn't just try to deal with the symptoms.

At some point, it would be wise to consider moving so your body can heal. The same is true for our souls. If your environment is making you unwell emotionally and psychologically, it may be time to remove yourself so you can heal. If you find yourself in this situation, I strongly advise seeking out a professional psychologist or counsellor who can offer support and suggestions for a way forward.

DON'T RETALIATE

> "Those who are servants, submit to the authority of those who are your masters—not only to those who are kind and gentle but even to those who are hard and difficult. You find God's favour by deciding to please God even when you endure hardships because of unjust suffering. For what merit is it to endure mistreatment for wrongdoing? Yet if you are mistreated when you do what is right, and you faithfully endure it, this is commendable before God. In fact, you were called to live this way, because Christ also suffered in your place, leaving you his example for you to follow. He never sinned and he never spoke deceitfully.
>
> When he was verbally abused, he did not return with an insult; when he suffered, he would not threaten retaliation. Jesus faithfully entrusted himself into the hands of God, who judges righteously." (1 Peter 2:18-23 TPT)

The apostle Peter calls us to stay true to our identity in Christ, refusing to retaliate in the face of abuse and mistreatment. Jesus was falsely accused, beaten, tortured, and finally killed, but He didn't sin. He didn't lie, didn't abuse, or threaten harm. Instead, Jesus stayed within the boundaries of righteousness and the Kingdom of God. He didn't resort to using the Kingdom of darkness's methods of self-protection but entrusted Himself to the Father.

It's easy to justify ungodly behaviour when experiencing the impact of ungodly behaviour from others. Jesus gives us another way; we never have to resort to Satan's ways to protect ourselves. When we feel powerless, we have a just and all-powerful God watching over us.

Jesus trusted His Father, the Righteous Judge. When we take judgment into our hands, we step outside the parameters set by God. In my practice, I use a parenting metaphor to illustrate the point. I have two boys who loved to wrestle when they were kids. Being children, they tended to execute justice on one another when their play got out of hand. If one got hit, retaliation was swift. They soon discovered that they both came under judgment because they'd both violated our family rule. The justification was predictable, "Well, he started it!"

My response was also predictable. "Well, you should have come to me. I would have judged the situation and issued some discipline to the one who had done wrong."

Children don't have the maturity or authority to execute justice righteously. It's the same in the Kingdom of God. God has the role of judging, and He will do it fairly and with love. If we revile and retaliate when people sin against us, we place ourselves outside Kingdom boundaries. When we seek justice, we can hinder God's righteous judgment in the situation.

When threatened, we naturally look to protect ourselves, and we have two choices, God's way or Satan's. There are only two kingdoms; anytime we act in a way that is not of God's Kingdom, we're ultimately doing it Satan's way.

Jesus shows us how disciples are to respond to a harsh leader. Our natural reaction may be to repay like for like and no longer respect their leadership. Of course, we're free to respond as we choose, but when we recognise that we have been mistreated and decide to lay it before the Lord, we inherit a blessing.

DISCERNING BETWEEN SUBMISSION AND BOWING TO INTIMIDATION

We need the wisdom to discern the difference between Godly authority and the voice of intimidation if we're to submit. In my marriage, there was an instance where I believed God wanted me to do something Ray didn't support. I was torn, but I gave it up when my husband voiced displeasure. You may imagine my surprise when I continued to feel the Lord lead me in the other direction. I kept laying it down, and each time, I felt God's pull towards the project. This continued until, eventually, the Lord spoke to Ray, and he changed his mind.

A few days later, I heard God whisper, "Now it's time to let it go and do what Ray wanted." It floored me. I'd endured an emotional and relational battle to hold on to something I thought was important to God. Now He was telling me to give it up. It didn't make any sense. When I questioned Him, He replied, "Now you're choosing out of love, not fear."

His words went right through me. I hadn't recognised I was in fear. Each time I'd decided to submit, it wasn't out of a heart of faith and love; it was to avoid the consequences of disappointing my husband. Ray's anger and disapproval rocked me emotionally. I felt like a bad wife and mother, and the path of least resistance was to yield to his request. True submission is given freely, not forced. It's not an escape route from pressure exerted by another person.

If we don't feel emotionally or physically safe to be our authentic selves, set appropriate boundaries, or speak our truth, we're under intimidation and, likely, manipulation. In other words, we're walking in self-protection, not love, and contrary to God's nature and best for us. He understands and doesn't condemn us, but we need to take steps to continue our walk into freedom.

THE COVENANT ABOVE ALL ELSE?

It's true; God doesn't like divorce. He knows the pain of separation for husbands, wives, and certainly for children. God is love, so anything that breaks a love covenant and brings pain or harm is not His desire for us. However, we must ensure that keeping marriages together doesn't become the highest goal while tolerating abuse.

The covenant may already be broken while a couple lives under the same roof. God looks at the heart, and it's hugely damaging when we make an idol out of marriage to the point of turning a blind eye to abuse and domestic violence.

> *"Since many faith communities place the intact family on a pedestal, religious women are especially prone to blame themselves for the abuse, believe they have promised God to stay married until death, and experience both the fear and reality of rejection at church when attempts to repair the relationship fail."* [2]

Many stories are surfacing of Christian women who reported domestic violence to their pastors or church leaders only to be told that to please God, they should stay and submit to their husbands. Unfortunately, many pastors and leaders have placed a high value on keeping the family unit together at all costs, sending a message that suffering abuse, forgiving, and praying for change is the best way.

But there are times when we must draw a line in the sand and say with our actions, not just our words, "This is wrong, and I will not tolerate this treatment any longer." We all get to decide what behaviour we accept and reject. It's *never* wrong to choose to protect yourself and your children from abuse. When the words and actions of another person impact our emotional, physical, and psychological wellbeing, safety comes first.

I once counselled a woman who was powerful and independent when she married. She was a pastor and enjoyed a very close relationship with God. However, after several years in an abusive marriage, her sense of self was crumbling. She blamed herself for how her husband treated her, believing she was the problem because he said so. This once confident woman was now ashamed and insecure. She spoke of feeling trapped, knowing the stigma attached to divorce in her church community. These factors contributed to her tolerating the abuse and changing herself rather than confronting his behaviour.

Eventually, she saw his behaviour for what it was, took decisive action, and moved out. She informed him she wouldn't be back unless he addressed his abusive behaviour. They were separated for several months, and during this time, she gained strength and perspective. The self-blame and shame gave way to recognition there was no justification for his verbal abuse and that he was responsible for his actions. She realised she didn't need to be perfect to deserve respect; she had a right to feel valued and safe in her home.

Thankfully, in this instance, my client's husband accepted responsibility for his anger and abusive behaviour and took the necessary steps to change. Her decision to walk away from the abuse challenged him to decide if he wanted to embrace healing and change or remain the same. She exercised her free will, decided what she would and would not accept, and likewise, her husband was free to choose and live with the consequences.

YOU CAN'T SURRENDER WHAT YOU DON'T HAVE

Refusing to tolerate abuse is about loving and valuing ourselves. The less worthy of love and respect we believe we are, the more prone we are to accepting mistreatment. It's easy to spiritualise our dysfunction and gravitate to laying down our rights for the good of others, becoming a martyr. I did this for many years. When I first became a Christian, I liked the idea of laying down my life, surrendering my rights and turning the other cheek. I thought the Christian life was straightforward and didn't understand why others struggled to do the same.

However, as I received healing from shame and feelings of inadequacy, the more uncomfortable I became. I finally understood that you couldn't surrender your rights if you didn't believe you deserved them in the first place. You need to accept your value and rights and then offer them *to Jesus*. When submitting stems from brokenness, it's not what God wants. You can't give something away you don't believe belongs to you.

When Jesus washed the feet of the disciples, He didn't believe he was unworthy or inadequate; He did it because he loved them.

> "Now Jesus was fully aware that the Father had placed all things under his control, for he had come from God and was about to go back to be with him. So he got up from the meal and took off his outer robe, and took a towel and wrapped it around his waist. Then he poured water into a basin and began to wash the disciples' dirty feet and dry them with his towel." (John 13:3-5 TPT)

Notice how this passage starts with a reminder Jesus knew who He was. He washed the disciple's feet in His full identity as the Son of God. We're called to humble ourselves and serve from a place of strength, identity, and significance. The first step is to know who we are and whose we are. Then, as we heal from our broken identity, we learn to stand in a place of strength, trusting in the Father, and drawing from love as we yield our rights and desires.

Jesus laid down His life willingly; no one took it from Him. It was His to keep or give, and He had the freedom to choose. So if yielding, serving, surrendering, and submitting feel like they're not optional for you, you're not able to freely give from a place of love.

> "This is how we have discovered love's reality: Jesus sacrificed his life for us. Because of this great love, we should be willing to lay down our lives for one another." (1 John 3:16 TPT)

We all need to learn who we are and accept our rights before we think about yielding and surrendering them. There is a time for everything in God; there are seasons, and recognising the one you're in and what God is building in you requires wisdom.

FORGIVENESS VS BOUNDARIES

As we've already discussed, it's not uncommon for women who report domestic violence to church leaders to be told to 'forgive and submit'. While forgiveness is a central teaching of the Bible, there's a big difference between forgiving and loving someone and tolerating abusive behaviour. You can love and forgive them from a safe distance while establishing boundaries that require a change of conduct before restoring the relationship.

Forgiveness within marriage is essential. When someone hurts or lets us down, we can feel they owe us. When Jesus taught on forgiveness, He explained it in terms of monetary debt. We are holding something against the person because of the price we've paid for their actions. We might say things like, "they owe me an apology". Forgiveness is the choice to release the debt, to wipe the slate clean. We let go of anger toward the person who hurt us and tear up the scorecard of wrongs against us.

Forgiveness isn't easy; it wars against our desire for justice and vindication. But it's truly an act of faith and a heart transaction. Forgiveness doesn't require anything from the offending person, and it doesn't mean that trust is restored. *Forgiveness is a gift, while trust must be earned.* Scripture commands us to forgive, but we're not commanded to trust. When trust is broken, relationships take time to rebuild. Likewise, forgiveness doesn't mean overlooking or tolerating abusive behaviour and not requiring change.

Sometimes we must put boundaries to prevent ongoing damage to ourselves and our families. We can walk in forgiveness and love and require those we're in a relationship with to treat us respectfully. Forgiveness doesn't mean engaging in the relationship as if the offence never happened. That may result from forgiveness, but it's not a requirement.

For example, if I own a business and a staff member steals from me, I can choose to forgive them and let go of any resentment and anger toward them. I may, however, decide that I will no longer put them in a position where they could steal from me again. Forgiveness doesn't negate the natural consequences of our actions.

Many women tell me that when they've talked to their husbands about hurtful behaviour and pushed for change, they were told they were at fault and to forgive the perceived wrong. The responsibility for resolving conflict in the relationship is placed on the one wronged with no accountability or consequences for the offender.

It's essential for our wellbeing that we feel emotionally and physically safe in marriage. Abusive relationships erode our sense of identity. Abuse also diminishes our ability to walk in our spiritual authority as believers. As I've already stated, your safety is paramount! Before putting boundaries in place, you must consider whether you will be emotionally and physically safe. If you're unsure, enlist the help of a professional who can offer support, strategies, and wisdom to lead you into change safely. I've listed some support organisations in the appendix that can help you develop a safety plan and work with you to achieve your goals safely.

I've experienced first-hand the freedom that comes from trusting God and following His lead. The Bible says it was for freedom that Christ set us free; if that's His intention for us, then it's possible. There may be different paths to freedom, but be assured that God desires to lead you out of oppression and into freedom, whatever that looks like for you. For the children of Israel, it meant waiting for their deliverer—Moses—to come on the scene. They watched the wrestle unfold between him and Pharoah and found the courage to follow him out of Egypt and into the wilderness.

Prayer

Father, thank you for your plan for marriage. Show me if there is anywhere I've surrendered my authority in my marriage. Please set me free from lies that have made me susceptible to manipulation or intimidation. I choose to walk in the authority you gave me and ask for help to do it freely and in love. Father, align me with your best for my marriage. I ask for a greater release of unity, love, and wisdom so we can go from strength to strength and glory to glory in our relationship. In Jesus' Name, Amen.

CHAPTER NINE

Eve in the Promised Land

The Israelites were in Egypt for 430 years, and they spent most of it enslaved. That's a long time, but there came the day God delivered them. He led them out victoriously—they even plundered the Egyptians. There's a principle in Scripture of recompense; when something is lost or stolen, it must be repaid-with interest (Numbers 5:5). God is taking us out of Egypt and into the Promised Land, from oppression and religion into His Kingdom.

Walking from religion into freedom takes courage. It's scary to step into unknown territory. Religion fences us in with lies to keep us captive in Egypt. But, again, we rely on the truth of God's love and nature, so we dare to leave. And while it's hard at first, it's also exhilarating. This is where our faith comes alive, where we find out what it means to be a Christian and what it looks like to be free.

I have talked with many Christians who believed God would not be with them if they stepped outside religious rules and structures. They feared losing their salvation or, at the very least, missing their calling. I've been there too.

There was a time when I was so scared of stepping outside God's protection that I submitted every aspect of my life to my pastor's authority. God gave me a vision for a Christian community-based counselling centre, so I sought my pastor's approval. I believed it was a church ministry; however, the pastor felt it should be something Ray and I ran independently of the church. Even after he told us, I kept submitting everything involving the centre to his authority. I'd heard so much teaching that as a congregation, we were to support the pastor's vision and that having a separate vision was wrong that I got confused. With an over-emphasis on such teaching, I lost the perspective that I could have my own vision and calling.

My poor pastor must have thought I was crazy! One day, fearful and confused, I asked the Lord, "Who is my spiritual covering?" He replied, "I Am". I realised I was so entrenched in my church's culture that I'd lost sight of my personal Kingdom authority and calling. It was a challenging season as I struggled to break free from my wrong beliefs around healthy submission to Godly authority.

The good news is that even when we make mistakes, God is a good Father and will never forsake us. Stop for a moment. Do you believe it? Jesus said He leaves the ninety-nine to find the lost one. You matter to God, and He'll come looking for you even if you walk away. He pursues you relentlessly with His love. Your part is to learn to rest in the security of His love, knowing He'll guide you back onto His path for your life.

GUARD YOUR HEART

> "So above all, guard the affections of your heart,
> for they affect all that you are.
> Pay attention to the welfare of your innermost being,
> for from there flows the wellspring of life."
> (Proverbs 4:23 TPT)

Most importantly, we must protect our relationship with God by guarding our hearts. I learned this lesson well when I shut my heart down to God after marrying Ray. The Lord knows our capacity to trust Him. He doesn't expect more from us than we're able to give, and He's not comparing you to others. Maintaining a soft heart toward Him is key to hearing His voice. Unresolved disappointments, hurts, and fears can cause our hearts to become hardened to the Holy Spirit, but He will show you anything that needs to be resolved if you ask Him to.

Take care not to allow abuses of authority to take you to a place where you despise all authority. Instead, keep seeking the heart of God through prayer and the Bible until you catch the true glory of His ways. True Kingdom authority is a blessing to everyone.

The essence of Kingdom relationships is beautifully portrayed in marriage, where partners choose to submit to and prefer one another. It translates to every sphere of relationship; between leaders and followers in the Kingdom and God Himself. We are the bride of Christ, and we're to love Him with all our hearts. Jesus sacrificed His life to empower and protect us, and our response is to lay down our lives as we care for people. We do these things willingly in the Kingdom out of gratitude and love, not law and fear. Our choice to submit to Kingdom authority never takes away our God-given authority. There's a balance to be struck, and the fruit of the Spirit marks it; when we find it—love, joy, and peace will result. Remember, in the Kingdom; it's about the heart, not behaviour!

CROSSING OVER

As you move towards Egypt's border, there's usually opposition. You may start second-guessing yourself or have well-meaning Christians counsel you to turn back. Don't worry; you're not going crazy! This is when we make decisions about whose voice we follow. You know His voice, and there's no need to fear the wrestle; it's part of leaving religion behind, strengthening yourself in God, and stepping into your authority as a child of the King.

The Lord once told me that it's the very process of *leaving* Egypt that prepares us to defeat the giants and enter the Promised Land. God's warriors need to be able to stand in what God says, even when others don't see it. That doesn't mean we isolate ourselves and not allow others to speak into our lives. God will bring one or two people alongside you to confirm what you're hearing. If you don't have those people, ask God for them. If He doesn't send them, press the pause button. God confirms things by two or three witnesses because He wants us to live in true fellowship.

KNOWING AND TRUSTING THE VOICE OF GOD IS IMPERATIVE.

> "And when he has brought out all his sheep, he walks ahead of them, and they will follow him, for they are familiar with his voice." (John 10:4 TPT)

When we hear God's voice, there's the witness of the Holy Spirit in us. You may have been taught untruths about Him or His ways, but deep in your spirit, you know His voice. God *is* love, and His voice is the sound of love. When you know someone well, you recognise their voice. The Father sounds like love, joy, peace, patience, kindness, goodness, and faithfulness, reflecting His nature.

Healing and truth go hand in hand. If you're struggling to recognise the voice of truth, it may be that your heart needs healing. Encountering His presence with the help of an anointed prayer minister is one way to accelerate healing and growth. It's not that the Lord is distant or not speaking, but the walls we build around our hearts to protect us from pain also reduce our sensitivity to hear Him. I encourage all believers to seek healing for their hearts; there is always more truth to be received.

Many of my clients begin a session saying they can't sense God or hear Him speak. But, by the end of our time, they've experienced Him in a beautiful, tangible way. Think of it like finding a radio station; sometimes, we need help filtering out the world's white noise so we can tune into His frequency.

It's time to shake off the false beliefs and religious mindsets that have kept us in oppression. No matter what we've done or experienced, Jesus has taken the guilt and shame and exchanged it for His righteousness. Let it go! Embrace the truth of who you are as a beloved daughter of God. You are His masterpiece, and the Father wants to bring you into wide-open spaces of freedom so the world can see His glory through you.

The religious doctrines that have tricked you into surrendering your authority have been exposed. Put them to death. Don't keep them in your back pocket 'just in case', but let the truth settle in your heart and mind. Pursue truth with all you have. Jesus promised that whatever you ask, it shall be given (John 14:13). He'll provide you with the desires of your heart, so as you make His truth your desire, He'll continue to expose the lies seeking to keep you captive.

RECLAIMING YOUR AUTHORITY

Reclaiming your authority is about exchanging the slave mentality for your identity as a daughter of God. It's time to agree with who He says you are and step into your authority. The parable of the lost son holds rich wisdom for us as we contemplate what it means to leave behind oppression and walk in our true authority as daughters of the King. In this story, the son walked away from His relationship with his father. He lived sinfully and squandered his inheritance through careless living. You can understand why he felt unworthy of being considered a son. While he eventually decided to return to his father, shame caused him to lower his gaze and think of himself as a servant instead of an heir.

"Humiliated, the son finally realised what he was doing, and he thought, 'There are many workers at my father's house who have all the food they want with plenty to spare. They lack nothing. Why am I here dying of hunger, feeding these pigs, and eating their slop? 18 I want to go back home to my father's house, and I'll say to him, "Father, I was wrong. I have sinned against you. I'll never again be worthy of being called your son. Please, Father, just treat me like one of your employees." (Luke 15:17-19 TPT)

When we choose to partake of the tree of the knowledge of good and evil, religion and shame partner to distort our perception of position. Even after turning back to God, we may feel unworthy of being reinstated as daughters clothed in dignity and carrying authority. Like the prodigal son, we assume the position of slaves who must earn their keep. In contrast, a daughter has access to everything that belongs to the Father because it's her birthright. It's simply her relationship to the Father that bestows honour and grants access to the resources of Heaven. An inheritance isn't earned; it's gifted out of relationship, not performance. The Father says that no matter what you've done, He will reinstate your full identity and authority as His beloved daughter.

I love how the father in the parable ignores the son's impassioned speech about his unworthiness. Instead, his focus is on restoring the son to his position. Finally, the father embraces him, calling for the items of clothing that confirm and communicate his identity as a son and heir.

Moving from a slavery mindset is pivotal as we take back our authority. A slave has no choice; they must do as they're told or face the consequences. A daughter, on the other hand, has options. She has access to her father's wisdom, resources, love, and the freedom to make decisions. She spends time with the Father and knows His ways. As she allows her new heart, filled with the Holy Spirit, to lead her, she becomes a liberator just like her Father.

> "The mature children of God are those who are moved by the impulses of the Holy Spirit. And you did not receive the "spirit of religious duty, leading you back into the fear of never being good enough. But you have received the "Spirit of full acceptance," enfolding you into the family of God. And you will never feel orphaned, for as he rises up within us, our spirits join him in saying the words of tender affection, "Beloved Father!" For the Holy Spirit makes God's fatherhood real to us as he whispers into our innermost being, "You are God's beloved child!" (Romans 8:14-16 TPT)

When we're born again into the family of God and filled with His Spirit, He leads us from the inside. Religion imposes rules from the outside to govern our behaviour, but that's not the Gospel. We're part of God's family and one with the Father, Son, and Holy Spirit. We learn to yield to the Holy Spirit and mature in His ways, just as a child learns from her parents. Children grow in wisdom and are incrementally given more and more freedoms by their parents. God's nature is being formed in you, and He wants you to discover the freedom available to you.

> "I am convinced that any suffering we endure is less than nothing compared to the magnitude of glory that is about to be unveiled within us. The entire universe is standing on tiptoe, yearning to see the unveiling of God's glorious] sons and daughters! For against its will, the universe itself has had to endure the empty futility resulting from the consequences of human sin.
>
> But now, with eager expectation, all creation longs for freedom from its slavery to decay and to experience with us the wonderful freedom coming to God's children. To this day we are aware of the universal agony and groaning of creation, as if it were in the contractions of labour for childbirth.
>
> And it's not just creation. We who have already experienced the first fruits of the Spirit also inwardly groan as we passionately long to experience our full status as God's sons and daughters—including our physical bodies being transformed." (Romans 8:18-24 TPT)

When the sons and daughters of God fully embrace their identity, freedom, and authority, they will liberate all creation. It's time to take back what was stolen in the Garden of Eden and release the Earth from slavery and oppression. We are to partner with His plan of redemption for the Earth. Everything flows from His Spirit. He is in us, and we are in Him; it's Christ in us, the hope of glory and our inheritance.

EVE ON THE RISE

Just as the Children of Israel made the journey from slavery in Egypt to possess their inheritance in the Promised Land, the daughters of Eve are on a journey from shame to glory. Isaiah 61:7 promises us recompense, a double portion for our shame. The time is now. There's a shift taking place, and God is setting us free from our oppressors. He's bringing revelation and insight so we can break agreement with the things that have kept us captive, freeing us to rise in freedom and glory.

Our Father is the God of justice; He had your redemption and rise planned before Eve took the bait. Regardless of what you've been through, God has made provision for your journey to the Promised Land. It's time to take back your authority. It's time to cross over. God is leading us out of Egypt and bringing us to Himself. He's inviting us to draw close in the wilderness and live from our intimacy with Him. When we spend time in His presence and see His glory, false beliefs are replaced with the truth. His truth brings the courage we need to enter the Promised Land. It's time to rise!

> "Arise [from the depression and prostration in which circumstances have kept you—rise to a new life]! Shine (be radiant with the glory of the Lord), for your light has come, and the glory of the Lord has risen upon you!" (Isaiah 60:1 AMP)

To *arise* is to stand up. It's a position of strength and boldness. In the Scripture, Isaiah is prophesying to Israel regarding their redemption and God's coming rescue from their current state of captivity in Babylon. So if you tell someone to "arise and shine", you're inviting them to be seen, to step out of the place of powerlessness and fear, into a position of authority and confidence.

Isaiah urges the Israelites to arise, even though their circumstances hadn't yet changed. He challenged them to change the way they viewed themselves and their situation. He reminds them of who they are and to whom they belong. In essence, Isaiah says, "Yes, you've been through captivity, oppression by your enemies, and you've felt shamed. But get up, today is the beginning of a new season, and you need to be reminded of who you really are!"

It's time to get up and take your place. There's a space God has allocated to each one in both the spiritual and natural realms. Taking your place in the spiritual realm means standing in your God-given authority and refusing permission for shame to keep you hidden. When we allow others to control us through manipulation or intimidation, we relinquish our authority. It's time to take it back so we can step fully into our God-given destiny. We have a part to play in His redemptive plan, and your gifts and anointing are required to liberate the Earth.

He created you to shine with His glory and occupy your space unashamedly. You may have to nudge people or spiritual beings out of the way but know that you have the Father's blessing. For too long, shame kept us hidden when God created us to shine. You are His masterpiece, and He wants you on display. There's a warrior inside you chomping at the bit to be released.

When God responded to the serpent in the Garden of Eden and dished out consequences for eating from the tree, He said that He would put enmity between the snake and the woman. This is a consequence for the snake, not the woman. The hostility wasn't a punishment for Eve; it was a punishment for Satan. Don't you love it? Women have been given a unique role in destroying Satan's works and Kingdom. This is our time! Women have had years of oppression in Egypt, but the tables have turned, and recompense is here. We're taking back our authority and using it to plunder the Kingdom of darkness.

Satan fears women, and he's sought to oppress and contain them ever since the days of Eve. He attempted to crush us and cause a slavery mentality to diminish our potency. And now, the enmity between the devil and women is culminating in his defeat.

In *Fashioned to Reign*, Kris Vallotton says,

> *"I think it is important to point out here that although the devil hates mankind, the spear point of spiritual warfare is womanhood!"*[1]

I have the privilege of praying with many Godly women. These warriors carry the love and heart of God as they pray for His Kingdom to come. They wrestle in prayer against principalities and powers and display fearlessness that comes from knowing their God-given authority.

We know Jesus is the ultimate offspring of Eve who would crush Satan's head, but God has given each of us a role in defeating the enemy. You were born for this exact moment in history. The gifts He's placed within you and the desires He placed in your heart will work for the liberation of all the Earth.

The world is waiting for you!

Prayer

Father, thank you for taking me out of shame and into glory. Thank you for the gifts and dreams You've given me. Thank you that I get to be a part of your plan to undo the devil's works and release creation from oppression. Father, I ask for new lenses to see me as You do. Give me the boldness and courage to step fully into all you have for me. I choose to embrace my identity as a daughter of the Most High God. I choose to take up my authority to rule and reign with Christ. In Jesus' Name, Amen.

Appendix

Domestic Violence

Domestic violence is any abusive behaviour used by one partner or family member in a relationship to gain and maintain control over another's life. It can occur in any type of domestic relationship, including spousal relationships, intimate personal relationships, family relationships and informal care relationships. There may be multiple perpetrators and victims within the household.

In 1948 the United Nations formed the Universal Declaration of Human Rights. So when we talk about abuse, we are talking about behaviour that violates our rights.

DECLARATION OF HUMAN RIGHTS

- Everyone is born free and equal in dignity and with rights.
- You should not be discriminated against for any reason. Rights belong to all people.

- Everyone has the right to life, liberty, and security.
- No one shall be held in slavery or servitude.
- No one shall be subjected to torture or to cruel, inhumane or degrading treatment or punishment.
- You have a right to be treated as a person in the eyes of the law.
- You have the right to protection by the law against violations of your rights.
- No one shall be subject to arbitrary arrest, detention, or exile.
- You have the right to freedom of movement within your country. Everyone has the right to leave a country and return home.
- Men and women have the same rights when they are married and when they are separated.
- You have the right to own property, and it cannot be taken away from you.
- You have the right to express those beliefs in teaching, practice, and worship.
- You have the right to freedom of opinion and expression.
- You have the right to freedom of peaceful assembly and association.
- You have the right to take part in the government of your country.
- As a member of society, you have a right to social security.
- You have the right to work, to good working conditions and to equal pay for equal work.
- You have the right to rest and leisure.
- You have the right to a decent life, including enough food, clothing, housing, medical care, and social services.
- You have the right to an education.
- No one may prevent you from participating in the cultural life of your community.
- You have the right to live in the kind of world where your rights and freedoms are respected. (United Nations, 2020)[1]

If you need help

- 1800RESPECT   Call 1800 737732   1800respect.org.au
- LIFELINE   Call 131114   Lifeline.org.au
- SAFE STEPS   Call 1800 015188   safesteps.org.au

NOTES

Introduction
1. William Wallace, as quoted at https://www.inspiringquotes.us/author/4557-william-wallace
2. *Oppression*, retrieved from https://www.merriam-webster.com/dictionary/oppression
3. Bevere, J. *Breaking Intimidation*. Lake Mary: Charisma House, 1995, 23
4. Ibid., 23
5. Al-Modallal, H. (2016). Childhood Maltreatment in College Women: Effect on Severe Physical Partner Violence. *Journal Of Family Violence*, 31(5), 607-615.
6. Australian Bureau of Statistics,. *Personal Safety Study 2016*. Australian Bureau of Statistics, 2017
7. Al-Modallal, H. *Childhood Maltreatment in College Women: Effect on Severe Physical Partner Violence. Journal Of Family Violence*, 2016, 31(5), 607-615.
8. Strathopoulos, M. *Sexual revictimisation: Individual, interpersonal and contextual factors. Australian Centre for the Study of Sexual Assault*, 2014
9. Benstead, U. (n.d.). *Shark Cage Group Program Manual*. PP Psychology Press, 2011, 17, 70-76

Chapter One: From Eve to Egypt
1. *Kingdom*, retrieved from https://www.merriam-webster.com/dictionary/kingdom
2. *Tree of Life* definition, Strong, J. *Strong's Exhaustive Concordance*, 1980
3. *Lord it over*, retrieved from https://www.thefreedictionary.com/lord+it+over
4. *Submission*, retrieved from https://www.dictionary.com/browse/submission

Chapter Two: Religion Kills
1. *Oppress*, definition, Strong, J. *Strong's Exhaustive Concordance*, 1980

Chapter Four: Freedom from Control
1. *Manipulation*, retrieved from https://dictionary.cambridge.org/dictionary/english/manipulation)
2. Anderson, Neil T, *Victory over the Darkness, Realising the power of your identity in Christ*, Bethany House, Video Seminar 2020

Chapter Six: Freedom from Intimidation
1. Bill Johnson, "Strengthen Yourself in the Lord: How to Release the Hidden Power of God in Your Life", p.62, Destiny Image Publishers, 2007.

Chapter Seven: Realms of Authority
1. Bevere, J. (2001). *Under Cover*. Thomas Nelson. (Bevere, 2001)

Chapter Eight: Kingdom Marriages
1. Day, C. O. (2010, December). Integrated responses to domestic violence; Legally mandated intervention programs for male perpetrators. *Trends and Issues in crime and criminal justice*, 404, 1-8. Retrieved

August 24, 2017 from http://www.aic.gov.au/media_library/publications/tandi_pdf/tandi404.pdf
2. Nason-Clark, N. (2009). Christianity and the Experience of Domestic Violence: What does faith have to do with it? *Social Work & Christianity*, 379-393.

Chapter Nine: Eve in the Promised Land
1. Vallotton, K. (n.d.). *Fashioned to Reign,* Baker Publishing Group, 2013, 64

Appendix
1. United Nations. *Universal Declaration of Human Rights.* January 20, 2020 Retrieved from United Nations: https://www.un.org/en/universal-declaration-human-rights/

ABOUT THE AUTHOR

Wendy Hayes lives, works and plays in Melbourne, Australia. She's married to Ray and has two children, three stepchildren, 5 grandchildren with more on the way. Wendy Hayes is a professional Christian counsellor with a Master of Community Counselling and over a decade in private practice. Wendy has been in church leadership for 23 years, leading inner healing ministries and lecturing at Harvest Bible College. Wendy has a passion for seeing Christian women step out of shame and fear into all they are created to be.

To contact the author please visit

reviveministries.com.au
wendy@reviveministries.com.au

www.ingramcontent.com/pod-product-compliance
Lightning Source LLC
Chambersburg PA
CBHW060529100426
42743CB00009B/1474